I Can Cook, You Can Cook!

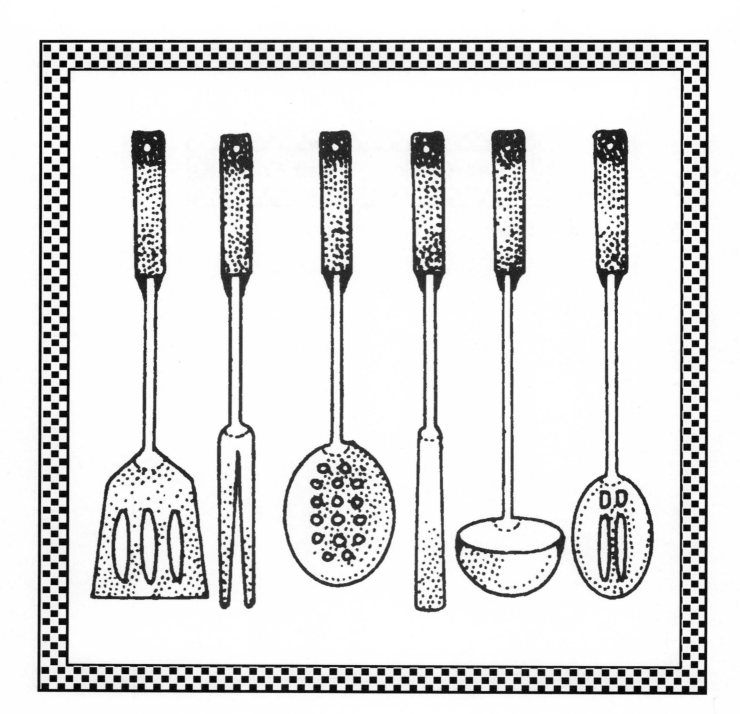

I Can Cook, You Can Cook!

SIMPLY GREAT MARYLAND RECIPES

Wayne Brokke

The Overlook Press
Woodstock & New York

First published in the United States in 2003 by
The Overlook Press, Peter Mayer Publishers, Inc.
Woodstock & New York

WOODSTOCK:
One Overlook Drive
Woodstock, NY 12498
www.overlookpress.com
[for individual orders, bulk and special sales, contact our Woodstock office]

NEW YORK:
141 Wooster Street
New York, NY 10012

Brokke, Wayne O. (Wayne Olaf), 1948-
I can cook, you can cook! : simply great Maryland recipes / Wayne O. Brokke.—1st edition
    p. cm.
ISBN 1-58567-440-0
1. Cookery, American. I. Title.
TX715.B849135 2003
641.5973—dc21
2003017167

Design by Charles Hames
Jacket photo by Edwin H. Remsburg

Manufactured in the United States of America

FIRST EDITION 2003
1 3 5 7 9 8 6 4 2
ISBN 1-58567-440-0

Acknowledgments

I would like to thank Brenda Eaton for her motivational support (nagging); Gregory, my twelve-year-old nephew, for being a taster (if he liked a recipe we knew the whole world would); Tamitra for being there; and Dean Smith for helping me write my introduction. Thanks also to Donna Hamilton at NBC's local station WBAL in Baltimore for her advice on how to make the book more personal. If you enjoy my stories, thank Donna; they became a part of this book because of her encouragement and creativity.

To Jim and Jay at DesignConcept for their patience and belief in the project, thank you. Many thanks to John Sheldon for pushing the book ahead; and to Robert Scholz for understanding why I didn't use any of the titles he suggested. Thank you to Steve and Lil Lanasa for more than twenty years of help and support. Thanks also to my aunts, C.C. Lewis and Sister M. Paulette (I am grateful my mother had two sisters). And lastly, to Dr. H, without whose guidance this book would not have been possible.

To the four people who edited, typed, and edited again, I am grateful: Nathan Snyder, Tracy Nunn, Jay Harris, and Yvette Young. May God bless.

A lovely lady named Karen Brooks inspired the title of this book. I went into a crab house with Gregory near my home. The woman behind the counter called out to me: "I can cook what you can cook!" she said. She began to tell the other customers how she didn't cook—that her husband took her to restaurants all the time. She then told us that she had written away for the recipes from my weekly TV cooking segment and that she could cook those. It made her look good in her husband's eyes. Over the next several months, Gregory would remind me what the crab lady had said. I told the story to Jay at DesignConcept. The next thing I knew we had decided on I Can Cook, You Can Cook!

Contents

Soups (*Continued*)

Salads

Entrees

Entrees (*Continued*)

Desserts

Author's Preface

Hi! My name is Wayne and I love to cook. It's fun for me and hopefully this cookbook will be fun for you. Learning to cook takes practice. It's a lifelong lesson in starting over. My sister Patricia once asked me how I get my prime rib medium rare. I replied that it took ten overcooked prime ribs before I got it right.

From mashed potato Easter eggs to Greek shrimp, *I Can Cook, You Can Cook!* features more than 150 recipes that are simple, fast, and easy to make. These recipes are not, however, written in stone. They are meant to be a guide for you to make up your own. If a recipe calls for a large onion and you don't like onion, take it out.

Good cooking for me is keeping things simple. It gives me comfort in a world that's complicated and constantly changing. In my kitchen, I can rely on the fact that a carrot will never disappoint me.

You can explore the world of cooking in many ways: take classes, read lots of cookbooks, or collect recipes from family and friends. Whichever path you take, do yourself a favor. Write down your family recipes before they are lost. They are part of your family tradition and collective memory, and that's too precious to let slip away.

And one more thing: don't be afraid to make mistakes.

How It All Got Started

MY first memory of cooking was when I was five years old. My mother was ill and I was standing on a stool over the stove with an open can of peas. I poured them into the pot. My family lived in Sparrows Point, a working-class neighborhood in the heart of Baltimore's steel making district. My brothers liked to play football and baseball. I liked to cook.

Four women in my family strongly influenced my passion for cooking. My grandmother Helen Doyas used to have all of us over for Sunday dinner. Her ham with pineapple glaze and chocolate covered macaroons will always remind me of her. Three large families would converge on her house and eat in shifts. Afterward, the adults played pinochle. It was a great family tradition.

My mother, Rose Brokke, had a flare for presentation. She used fine linens, silver, and pink roses from her garden on the mahogany table. Thanksgiving was spectacular: sauerkraut, turkey, stuffing, and kielbasa. Our front porch served as the refrigerator for her many creations. I remember the desserts—especially the Christmas cookies. Early in December, she'd start filling potato chip tins with oatmeal cookies, chocolate chips, and sugar cookies in the shapes of stars, angels, and snowmen. Those were wonderful times.

During the summer in our neighborhood, a street Arab named Benline, a produce vendor with a pony-drawn cart, would come by with fresh fruits and vegetables. He would yell, "cantaloupe, watermelon, strawberries!" My mother would make strawberry-rhubarb sauce that we'd pour over ice cream.

Maitresse Chester, my Aunt Mae, came every Sunday, sometimes unannounced. My mother would worry that we wouldn't have enough for everyone. Once through the door,

Aunt Mae would smile, "Come on Wayne, let's go into the kitchen." She would open up the fridge and we'd make something from whatever was in there. My mother didn't even know she had the ingredients for such wonderful dishes. . . .

My great aunt, Anna, lived close to our school in Highlandtown. She liked to cook flamboyant meals. We'd go to her house on our lunch break and have a seven-course gastronomic experience that ended with flaming crêpe suzettes. I was in fifth grade and had never seen fire inside a house before. She made peas and slaw in heaping portions. For some reason that is the dish I remember the most.

I was around adults a lot growing up. When my mother wasn't feeling well, I had to save my family from my father's cooking. He'd throw everything into the pot and sprinkle in barley—his version of soup du jour. So, from an early age, I did the cooking. My grandmother would teach me tricks like putting "magic crystals" on carrots. It was a while before I figured out it was just salt. My cooking mentors were always proud to show me their secrets.

Now, when I prepare a table and it looks good, I think of my mother. When something doesn't go well, I call on Aunt Mae and add something quickly to save the dish. Grandmother Helen keeps me straight on the communal dishes and mashed potato Easter eggs.

Recipes are guidelines, not the Ten Commandments. Use them to fit your own cooking needs. *I Can Cook, You Can Cook!* covers more than 100 years of ethnic cooking in Baltimore. Every recipe in this book—many transcribed and adapted from the handwriting of Helen, Rose, Anna, and Mae—has a memory attached to it. My mother always looked elegant when she cooked. She wore red lipstick, her fingernails were red, and her apron had cherries on it. Aunt Mae and I would make potato salad together. One Sunday we were missing celery, so she brought out a large jar of pickles. To this day, I use pickles in my potato salad.

During my youth, I cooked often for friends and family. I enjoyed it so much I opened a restaurant. We didn't have very many choices in Charm City back then. You could find a formal sit-down experience or eat at the corner bar. There were no casual restaurants in Baltimore, so I decided to open one. The Soup Kitchen Limited was the first restaurant of its kind in Baltimore. I started out with ten soup recipes and within a year had more than 300, from chicken noodle to sweet potato crab. I was in heaven. I'd go across Charles

Street to the Cross Street market and pick out the broccoli, spinach, and asparagus. Back in the kitchen, I'd reference three or four cookbooks and come up with my own creations. The customers loved it. For them and me it was instant gratification.

After a decade of soups, I decided to branch out. I went slowly at first, incorporating elements of Italian, Greek, and Spanish cooking. Then, the Orioles moved to Camden Yards and I knew I would need something for the best (and hungriest) fans in baseball. Baltimore had never heard of pulled pork or pulled chicken. Good spare ribs were unknown here. So, I went down to John Wayne's Barbecue in Lexington, North Carolina and got the best advice from the owner: "I don't care what you do with pork. You can baste it. You can boil it. You can roast it. The sauce is what counts." So I decided to call my restaurant Wayne's Bar-B-Que and make my own sauces.

A few years ago, I started cooking on television. My weekly segment on WBAL NBC Channel 11 has been a tremendously gratifying experience. Each and every time I go in front of the camera, I feel the presence of the four women who taught me to cook and it makes me smile.

Cooking to me should be easy, fast, and exciting. It's should also be about family coming together to share the experience. It's about the seasons and the meals you associate them with—the color combination of Maryland tomatoes, sweet corn, crab cakes, and ice tea with lemon slivers as the summer sun sets on the back porch. It's also about what sticks to our ribs and what keeps us stuck together. It's about enjoying a meal with good friends. . . .

I learned from my dear friend Herschel Caston the most important lesson of all: No matter how you cook, no matter how fancy your preparations may be, sharing the joy and pleasure of the company you keep is all that matters.

If I can cook, you can cook, OK? Bye!

Wayne

This book is dedicated to
Helen, Rose, Anna, and Mae

I Can Cook, You Can Cook!

Soups

Tuna Tomato Bisque

At The Soup Kitchen Limited, my first restaurant, one of the most popular soups was Cream of Tomato. Then one day there was a sale on tuna. I used my gift of creating one soup from another and presto chango! Tuna Tomato Bisque.

Serves 6–8

2–6 1/8 oz cans of tuna in water
2 cups chicken stock or 2 cups of water with 2 tsp of chicken bouillon granules (If soup is too thick, add more stock or half-and-half.)
1–28 oz can of fresh cut diced tomatoes or 1–28 oz can of whole tomatoes, hand-crushed
1/2 cup of onion, chopped
1/2 cup of carrots, sliced
1/2 cup of celery, sliced
1 cup of half-and-half
2 oz of butter, 1/2 stick
1/4 cup of flour
1 tsp of garlic powder or fresh, chopped
1 Tbsp of lemon juice
1 Tbsp of sugar
1/2 tsp of ground red pepper
1 Tbsp of Worcestershire sauce
Salt and pepper to taste

1. In butter, sauté onion, carrots and celery.
2. Add flour and cook for 3 minutes.
3. Next, add chicken stock.
4. Add garlic, ground red pepper, lemon juice, sugar and Worcestershire sauce.
5. Stir in tomatoes and allow to simmer for about 10 minutes.
6. Then, add half-and-half.
7. You can now stop and you have a wonderful cream of tomato. Salt and pepper to taste.
8. Add tuna and serve.

Wayne's hint ☞ Try one of the following: add broccoli, crabmeat, sliced mushrooms, or top with Feta cheese. Let your imagination be your guide.

Chicken Corn Chowder

This soup was inspired by many trips through Pennsylvania Dutch country. When making this soup, I prefer using yellow corn. I love white corn, which I believe is more tender and sweeter, however yellow corn, to me, has more of a corn flavor.

Serves 4–6

1 lb of boneless chicken breast, cut into 1–inch cubes
8 cups of chicken stock or 8 cups of water with 8 tsp of chicken bouillon granules
2 cups of corn, fresh or frozen, yellow or white (If you like corn as I do, add more.)
2 cups of white potatoes, peeled and cubed (I prefer Yukon Gold.)
1 cup of onion, chopped
1 cup of celery, cut into 1/8–inch slices
4 hard boiled eggs, chopped
1 tsp of Thyme
Salt and pepper to taste

1. Bring stock to a boil.
2. Add onions, thyme (If you are using fresh thyme, add it when you add the eggs.) and celery. Simmer until onions become translucent.
3. Next, add chicken. Continue cooking for 10 minutes.
4. Add potatoes and corn, cooking until potatoes are fork tender.
5. Then, add eggs.
6. Adjust seasoning with salt and pepper.
7. Cook over medium heat for another 10 minutes.

Wayne's hint ☞ Feel free to experiment with white or yellow corn or try a combination of the two. Both Gregory and Yvette love this soup, so I give it a four star rating.★★★★

Wayne's White Chili

White Chili came about one cold winter day when I received a phone call from a friend of mine. He needed a recipe for white chili. He was on one of his famous diets (you know the yo-yo). He thought chicken would make him thinner. To accommodate this passionate dieter and to help him with his commitment to shedding pounds, I told him I needed a little time and would call him back. I rushed to the store, bought chicken and white beans. I went right to work creating this recipe. I jotted down the ingredients and method, and then called and gave him this recipe which I guaranteed would shed pounds.

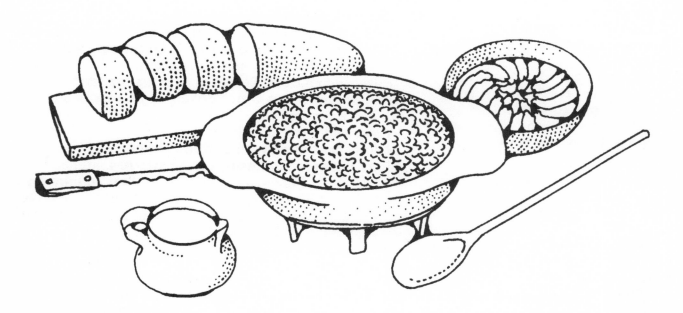

Serves 8–12

2–19 oz cans of white kidney
    beans (cannellini), drained
2 lbs of chicken breast, cubed
4 cups of chicken stock or 4 cups
    of water with 4 tsp of chicken
    bouillon granules
1 cup of onion, chopped
1 cup of celery, chopped
1 cup of green pepper, chopped
2 Tbsp of flour
1/4 tsp of dry mustard
2 tsp of cumin
2 tsp of garlic powder or fresh,
    chopped
1 Tbsp of chili powder
1/4 tsp of Cayenne pepper
1 tsp of cilantro
1 Tbsp of sugar
2 Tbsp of vegetable oil
2 tsp of Tabasco sauce
1–10 oz bag of Fritos
Salt and pepper to taste

1. In a soup pot, sauté celery, onions, and green
    peppers in oil.
2. Then add all spices, dry mustard, sugar and
    Tabasco. Sauté briefly.
3. Add flour and cook for about 3 minutes.
4. Next, add chicken stock.
5. Bring to a simmer then add chicken.
6. On medium heat, cook for 20 minutes.
7. Then, add beans and cook for another 10 minutes.
8. Adjust the seasoning with salt and pepper to taste.
9. Top with grated cheddar or pepper jack cheese and
    Fritos. Bobby you leave this step out.

Wayne's hint ☞ If you're not laughing by now, I am. I hope he is too. Needless to say, my friend's need for a healthier way of living brought about creativity, inspiration, perspiration, and humor. Ground chicken, ground turkey, or even leftover turkey can be used in place of chicken breast.

Strawberry Rhubarb Soup

When I was about seven or eight years old, I visited my grandpa Targy Brokke, who lived on a farm in North Dakota. Targy would give me a shaker of salt and tell me to go to the rhubarb patch and take a stalk, salt it, and eat it. This is how I became very fond of rhubarb, in addition to my fondness for listening to Grandpa play the fiddle.

Serves 4

6 stalks of rhubarb
2 pints of strawberries
1 cup of sugar
4 cups of water

1. **Wash and cut rhubarb into 1/2–inch slices. Set aside.**
2. **Take the tops off strawberries and cut in half. Set aside.**
3. **In a pot, bring sugar and water to a simmer.**
4. **Next, add rhubarb and strawberries.**
5. **Simmer for 30 minutes or until rhubarb is very tender.**
6. **Serve hot and top with sour cream or cold with whipped cream.**

Wayne's hint ☞ Don't be afraid to add more rhubarb and strawberries. The leaves of rhubarb are poisonous. The stalks will vary from a very dark ruby red to a light pink and slight green. The taste will be the same. When served cold this is great over ice cream.

P.S. Sometime I leave the strawberries out.

Cream of Mushroom Soup with Blue Cheese ▰▰▰▰▰▰

Serves 4–6

8 oz of mushrooms, coarsely chopped including the
    stems

8 oz of mushrooms, caps removed from stems and
    cut into 1/2 inch slices, reserve stems for
    chopping

1 cup of onion, chopped

4 oz of butter, 1 stick

4 oz of flour

3 cups of chicken stock or 3 cups of water with 3
    tsp of chicken bouillon granules

2 cups of half-and-half or whole milk

4 oz of blue cheese

1 Tbsp of Tabasco

Salt and pepper to taste

1. In butter, sauté onion. Then add chopped
    mushrooms.
2. Add flour and cook for 5 minutes, stirring
    constantly.
3. Then, slowly add chicken stock.
4. Next, slowly add milk or half-and-half.
5. Whisk until soup starts to thicken. Soup will not
    thicken until it comes to almost a boil.
6. Add Tabasco and sliced mushrooms.
7. Adjust seasoning with salt and pepper. Simmer for
    10 minutes.
8. Top with crumbled blue cheese.

Wayne's hint ☞ Remember, flour will act differently depending upon the time of year
and the type of flour used. So, if the soup is too thick, don't worry, just add more milk.

Wayne's Award Winning Maryland Crab Soup

Seven Time winner of the *Old Bay* ® *Soupstakes*,

Critic's, **and *People's Choice* Award**

I've been making this recipe for more than twenty-five years. My grandmother Helen Elizabeth Doyas passed it down to me. I believe she got it from our relatives on the Eastern Shore of Maryland (they owned a chicken farm), whom she would visit sometimes when she was mad at my grandfather—I called him Pop Pop.

Serves 8–10

4 quarts of water

1 lb of lump crab meat, fresh or frozen (If you want to add more crabmeat, feel free, it's your buck.)

1 lb of claw crabmeat, fresh or frozen

1/2 dozen soup crabs or 3 small live crabs, cleaned

1–28 oz can of whole tomatoes, hand crushed

1–28 oz can of crushed tomatoes

1 1/2 cups of chopped celery

1 1/2 cups onion, chopped

4 cups red potatoes, cubed, skin-on

1 1/2 cups of peas, fresh or frozen

1 1/2 cups of green beans, fresh or frozen

1 1/2 cups of corn, fresh or frozen

1 1/2 cups of Lima beans, fresh or frozen

1 1/2 cups of carrots, sliced and halved

1 1/2 cups of cabbage, chopped

2 Tbsp of Old Bay, or more to taste

2 bay leaves

2 Tbsp of beef base or bouillon granules

2 Tbsp of chicken base or bouillon granules

1/4 cup Worcestershire sauce

1 Tbsp of Tabasco sauce

2 Tbsp of sugar

Salt and pepper to taste

1. In a large soup pot, bring the water to a boil and then add the chicken and beef base or bouillon. Stir until dissolved.
2. Thoroughly rinse and clean the crab parts, cut them in half, add to the stock and bring to a second boil (skim any excess froth created by the crab parts).
3. Add sugar, Old Bay, bay leaves, Worcestershire sauce, Tabasco sauce and tomatoes. Simmer for 10 minutes.
4. Then add all other vegetables (excluding the potatoes) and cook for 10 minutes.
5. Add potatoes. Cook until fork tender.
6. Add crabmeat and cook for 10 minutes.
7. Adjust seasoning with salt and pepper.

Wayne's hint ☞ The broth is what makes this soup, and there are two items you absolutely must use in order to get the desired flavor: cabbage and fresh uncooked crab parts. You can decide what vegetables you like and which ones to use. But, remember the crabmeat alone will not give that authentic Maryland Crab Soup taste.

Wayne's Cucumber Soup ▨▨▨▨▨▨▨▨▨▨▨▨▨

From time to time over the years I've been asked when to serve cold soup. As a rule of thumb, I would usually serve cold fruit soups in place of dessert and cold vegetable soups in place of a salad. This particular soup is a great accompaniment to fish, chicken, or beef. I've served it many times with codfish cakes, a recipe that can be found later in this book.

Serves 4–6

4 cups of sour cream
4 cups of water
4 cups of cucumbers, forked, quartered and sliced very thin
1 Tbsp of dill, chopped fine, fresh, dried or frozen can be used
1 tsp of white pepper
1 tsp of salt

1. **Whisk sour cream and water together, making sure there are no lumps.**
2. **Add dill, salt and pepper, whisk and taste at this time to adjust seasoning.**
3. **Add cucumbers and chill for at least 2 hours before serving.**

Wayne's hint ☞ The combination of equal parts water to sour cream is a good base for other cold soups. As an example, add grated cucumbers and grated beets to this mixture, a dash of nutmeg, salt, and pepper. Makes for a wonderful borsch.

Broccoli Crab Soup

I had many favorite soups at The Soup Kitchen Ltd. This particular soup was the favorite of Mayor Schaefer (who later became governor of the great State of Maryland). Whenever he was preparing to go on a trip, his aides would call the restaurant and place an order for several containers of Cream of Broccoli Soup for him to take with him. Crabs are a way of life in Maryland, so adding crabmeat to this soup seemed like a good combination to me. I hope you feel the same way.

Serves 4–6

4 cups of chicken stock or 4 cups of water with 4 tsp of chicken bouillon granules
1 lb of crabmeat
1 lb of broccoli, fresh or frozen, chopped
1 cup of onion, chopped
1 Tbsp of curry powder
2 tsp of garlic powder or fresh, chopped
4 oz of margarine or butter, 1 stick
4 oz of all-purpose flour
2 cups milk or half-and-half
1 tsp of Tabasco
Salt and pepper to taste (Remember salt after using bouillon granules.)

1. **In a soup pot, sauté chopped onion in butter until translucent. Add curry powder and garlic.**
2. **On medium heat, add flour and stir until smooth, about 5 minutes.**
3. **Gradually add chicken stock and whisk constantly.**
4. **Bring almost to a boil. Add chopped broccoli and cook for 15 minutes.**
5. **Add half-and-half or milk. Allow to simmer.**
6. **Next, add Tabasco sauce.**
7. **Adjust seasoning to taste with salt and pepper.**
8. **Add crabmeat.**
9. **Allow to simmer for about 5–10 minutes. Serve.**

Wayne's hint ☞ Try other variations of this versatile soup by adding: 1 1/2 cups of cheddar cheese or 1 1/2 cups of chopped tomatoes.

Banana Bisque

At The Soup Kitchen Ltd. the first cold soup we had was Gazpacho. To my surprise people loved it. The demand for cold soups was unbelievable. This was during the 1970s when I had never even heard of cold soup. Within months of opening, cold soups were selling as well as hot soups. Banana Bisque was the first of many cold fruit soups that was created for this demand.

Serves 4

4 bananas, sliced
4 oz of pecans, finely chopped
1/2 tsp of almond extract
1/4 cup of dark rum
2 cups of half-and-half
1 Tbsp of powdered sugar (Depending on how sweet prefer, If you're like Yvette, the one that's typing the recipes, you'd put 2 maybe 3.)
1 cup of whipped cream or cool whip

1. **Place bananas in a blender.**
2. **Add rum, powdered sugar, almond extract and half-and-half.**
3. **Puree and then chill.**
4. **Top with whipped cream and chopped pecan.**

Wayne's hint ☞ I love to serve this soup as a dessert. Wouldn't it be nice on a hot summer night to have grilled chicken, Mediterranean potato salad, and, for dessert, banana bisque?

Cream of Spinach 5 Ways 　:■:■:■:■:■:■:■:■:■:■:■:■:■:■:■:

At The Soup Kitchen Ltd. one of top ten soups was Cream of Spinach. I've always been amazed that a recipe so simple could be so wonderful. This inspired me to create Crab Florentine by adding a pound of crabmeat. Oyster Florentine by adding a pint of oysters. By adding a pound of sliced mushrooms, you get Cream of Spinach Mushroom. Cream of Spinach with Feta and Tomato by adding 4 oz of Feta and a cup of chopped tomatoes. Once you've prepared this recipe, I think you'll be inspired too.

Serves 4–6

4 cups of chicken stock or 4 cups of water with 4 tsp of chicken bouillon granules
1 lb of spinach, chopped, fresh or frozen
1 cup of onion, chopped
1/2 tsp of nutmeg
1 Tbsp of garlic powder or fresh, chopped
4 oz of margarine or butter, 1 stick
4 oz of flour
2 cups of half-and-half
1 tsp of Tabasco
Salt and pepper to taste

1. **In a soup pot, sauté onion and garlic in butter until onion becomes translucent. Add nutmeg.**
2. **On medium heat, add flour and stir until smooth, about 5 minutes.**
3. **Gradually add chicken stock, whisking constantly.**
4. **Bring almost to a boil then add spinach.**
5. **Cook for about 15 minutes.**
6. **Add half-and-half; allow simmering.**
7. **Next add Tabasco sauce.**
8. **Adjust seasoning and serve.**

Wayne's hint ☞ Sometimes I like a thicker soup. If you prefer it thinner, just cut the butter and flour in half.

Gazpacho, Chilled Vegetable Soup ▪▫▪▫▪▪▫▪▫▪▫▪▫▪▪

My first try at making Gazpacho was not a success. In fact, it was a huge disaster. I was fairly new at making cold vegetable soups. Instead of using 2 cloves of garlic I used 2 heads of garlic. Please don't make this mistake. This soup was so garlicky it took me years to even think about Gazpacho again. That was over twenty-five years ago, and it's only recently that I have rediscovered this wonderful Spanish soup. The garlic mishap, thank God, has not been repeated. A lesson well learned.

Serves 4–6

6 cups of tomatoes, cubed
(approximately 3 large
tomatoes)
2 cups of cucumbers, skin-on and
cubed
1 cup of onion, chopped
1 cup of green pepper, stems
removed, seeded, and cubed
1 Tbsp of garlic powder or fresh,
chopped
1 1/2 cups of tomato juice
2 Tbsp of lemon juice
1/3 cup of red wine vinegar
1/2 cup of olive oil
2 tsp of sugar
1 tsp of white pepper
1 tsp of thyme
1 tsp of cilantro
1 tsp of cumin
1 tsp of cayenne pepper
Salt to taste

1. In a blender or food processor, place a combination of tomatoes, cucumbers, onions, and green peppers. You can choose between finely or coarsely chopped (This will depend on your taste). Tomato juice may be added during this step to help liquefy ingredients.
2. Remove to a large bowl. Continue this process until all vegetables have been through the blender.
3. Next, add to your blender tomato juice, lemon juice, red wine vinegar, olive oil, thyme, sugar, cilantro, garlic, cumin, cayenne pepper, and white pepper, blend for about 2 minutes.
4. Then, combine all ingredients into large mixing bowl, making sure to mix well.
5. Salt and pepper to taste.
6. Refrigerate for at least 2 hours.
7. Garnish with chopped green pepper, cucumber and tomato.

Wayne's hint ☞ For an extra treat, try adding lump crabmeat. You know what? Now that I think about it, with some crusty bread and a nice glass of dry white wine, this could be for one of those hot, sultry, summer lunches or dinners.

Irish Potato Stew

Serves 6–8

4 cups of potatoes, peeled and cubed
1 cup of onion, chopped
1 cup of celery, chopped
4 oz of butter, 1 stick
4 oz of flour
6 cups of chicken stock or 6 cups of water with 6 tsp of chicken bouillon granules
2 cups of half-and-half
1 bay leaf
1 tsp of Tabasco sauce
Salt and pepper to taste

1. Sauté onions and celery in butter until translucent.
2. Mix in flour and cook for 10 minutes, (this makes what is called a roux).
3. Next, add stock slowly until thick and smooth.
4. Add potatoes, bay leaf, salt and pepper.
5. Cook until potatoes are almost done.
6. Next, slowly add half-and-half. Simmer for 15 minutes.
7. Adjust seasonings and give a hearty sprinkle of Tabasco sauce.

Wayne's hint ☞ To add a little pizzazz to this dish, garnish with broccoli florets and shredded cheddar cheese or bacon. Wouldn't it be great to try all of the above?

Russian Cabbage (Wayne's All Time #1)

I love this soup. Eating it along with crusty bread, I am a happy camper. I've never been a fan of leftovers, but I could eat this soup for two or three days and still be happy. It was also a favorite of Mr. Sugar, a developer of shopping centers in the Baltimore/Washington area, who was a regular at The Soup Kitchen Ltd. He said it brought back warm memories of his grandmother, a Russian immigrant, who made this soup often.

Serves 6

4 cups of cabbage, shredded, very fine (not red)
1 cup of onion, chopped fine
1–28 oz can of crushed tomatoes
1/2 cup of brown sugar
2 cups of chicken stock or 2 cups of water with 2 tsp of chicken bouillon granules
2 cups of beef stock or 2 cups of water with 2 tsp of beef bouillon granules
1/2 cup of white vinegar
2 tsp of Tabasco
Salt and pepper to taste

1. **Bring stock to a boil.**
2. **Add onions, brown sugar, vinegar and Tabasco.**
3. **When onions are soft add cabbage and tomatoes.**
4. **Simmer for about 45 minutes to 1 hour or until cabbage is tender.**
5. **Adjust seasonings with salt and pepper.**

Wayne's hint ☞ The finer you chop your cabbage, the smoother your soup will be. You know what? I think it tastes even better.

Lentil Soup With Frankfurters and Black Olives

This is a meal in itself along with a salad and some wonderful bread. Just imagine a fall day when the soup bug has hit you—this is the soup. Do it! Do it! Do it! And enjoy.

Serves 6–8

1 lb of dried lentils
4 hot dog links, cut into 1/4–inch rounds (optional)
1 cup of sliced black olives (optional)
1 cup of onion, chopped
1 cup of celery, chopped
1/2 cup of carrot, chopped
8 cups of chicken stock or 8 cups of water with 8 tsp of chicken bouillon granules
2 Tbsp of olive oil
1 Tbsp of garlic powder or fresh, chopped
1 tsp of basil, dried
1 tsp of crushed red pepper
Salt and pepper to taste

1. **Wash and sort out lentils making sure there are no small pebbles.**
2. **In a soup pot, sauté in oil, garlic, onion, celery, and carrot for 5 minutes.**
3. **Add lentils and stock. Cook for about 1 hour.**
4. **Next, add red pepper and basil.**
5. **Add hot dogs and black olives and simmer for 10 minutes.**
6. **Adjust seasoning with salt and pepper and serve.**

Wayne's hint ☞ Mr. Dean and his girlfriend, Christina, whom everyone loves, have a tradition of making lentil soup on New Year's Day because it is a symbol of good luck in the New Year. When Gregory was about seven years old he said, "if Mr. Dean doesn't stop dating so many women, when I'm old enough to date there won't be anyone left for me." Mr. Dean stopped in the name of love. I think it was Christina's lentil soup that did the trick.

P.S. If you don't want the hot dogs and black olives, which I adore, try substituting 2 cups of tomatoes and 1/4 cup of fresh basil.

Sweet Potato Crab

This soup was inspired one cold winter day while walking through the Cross Street market (an old city market that in its heyday was the predecessor of the supermarkets of today). At one stall there were rows and rows of sweet potatoes piled on top of another, hundreds of them. And right next to that stall were bushels and bushels of crabs, alive and squirming. Somehow it looked to me like a match made in heaven. Of course, I think I had a hangover that morning (in fact, I did).

Serves 4–6

1 lb of backfin crabmeat
6 cups of sweet potatoes, peeled and quartered
1 cup of onion, chopped
4 cups of chicken stock or 4 cups of water with 4 tsp of chicken bouillon granules
2 cups of half-and-half
1 cup of orange juice (Use 1/2 cup if you would like it to be less sweet.)
2 tsp of marjoram
2 Tbsp of brown sugar (Don't tell Yvette we changed the amount.)
2 tsp of Tabasco
Salt and pepper to taste

1. **Bring stock to a boil.**
2. **Add sweet potatoes, onion, orange juice, brown sugar, marjoram and Tabasco.**
3. **Cook until sweet potatoes are done.**
4. **Put soup into a blender and puree.**
5. **Next, put puree back into pot and bring to a simmer.**
6. **Then, add crabmeat.**
7. **Slowly add half-and-half. Allow simmering for about 10 minutes.**
8. **Adjust seasonings with salt and pepper.**

Wayne's hint ☞ I have never used canned sweet potatoes in this recipe. Try it and let me know how it turns out. My website is waynecooks.com. We have to get a little plug in every now and then.

Knickerbocker Bean Soup

There are many different ways to make a bean soup. In my family there were two schools of thought. One being that you never add tomatoes and potatoes to your bean soup. The other was that you always add tomatoes and potatoes to your bean soup. I've always preferred using tomatoes and potatoes in my bean soup. Now I know you may be tired of my discussing tomatoes and potatoes in the bean soup, so what I did to stop this nonsense is to call this Knickerbocker Bean, which has tomatoes and potatoes in it.

Serves 6–8

1 ham hock
1 lb of dried navy beans
8 cups of chicken stock or 8 cups
  of water with 8 tsp of chicken
  bouillon granules
2 cups of potatoes, peeled and
  cubed
1 cup of onion, chopped
1 cup of celery, sliced
1 cup of carrots, sliced
1–28 oz can of whole tomatoes,
  hand crushed
1 Tbsp of dill, fresh, frozen or
  dried
 2 tsp of garlic powder or fresh,
  chopped
1 bay leaf
2 tsp of Tabasco
Salt and pepper to taste

1. **Rinse and sort beans in a large bowl or pot. Cover with water.**
2. **Let stand overnight or at least 4–6 hours, drain.**
3. **Bring chicken stock to a boil and add ham hock, making sure ham hock is well covered.**
4. **Reduce to a simmer and cook for 30 minutes.**
5. **Add onions, carrots, tomatoes, celery, dill, garlic, bay leaf and Tabasco.**
6. **Drain beans and add to pot. Simmer for 1 hour.**
7. **After 1 hour, add potatoes.**
8. **Simmer until beans are done and potatoes are fork tender. More hot water may be added if needed during cooking.**
9. **Adjust seasoning with salt and pepper.**

Wayne's hint ☞ Quick-soak bean method: Place rinsed and sorted beans in a pot and cover with water. Bring to a simmer. Remove from heat and let set for 1 hour, covered. Drain and use in your recipe as directed. Let me tell you something, the only difference between pre-soaked and no soak beans is the amount of time it takes to cook the soup. So, if the soup bug hits you at the last minute, you will just have to cook your beans a little longer. It's only about 1/2 hour.

Zucchini Stew

The abundance of zucchini is usually at its peak during the late summer and fall. However, you can buy zucchini all year round. If you grow your own and the plants start producing, you'll need as many zucchini recipes as you can find. I like this recipe a lot because I get tired of making ratatouille.

Serves 6

1 lb of Italian sweet sausage, par boiled, cooled and cut into 1/2 inch slices
3 cups of tomatoes, fresh or 1–28 oz can of whole tomatoes, hand crushed
2 cups of potatoes, cubed
2 cups of zucchini, quartered and cubed
2 Tbsp of olive oil
1 cup of onion, chopped
1/2 cup of celery, chopped
1 Tbsp of garlic powder or fresh, chopped
1/2 cup of parsley, chopped
1 Tbsp of basil, chopped (If it's fresh add at the end, if it's dried add when you sauté.)
2 cups of chicken stock or 2 cups of water with 2 tsp of chicken bouillon granules
Salt and pepper to taste

1. In a large pot, sauté celery, onion and garlic in oil until tender.
2. Next, add tomatoes and parsley. Simmer for 10 minutes.
3. Add potatoes and chicken stock. Cook for 10 minutes.
4. Then, add zucchini, sausage, and basil. Cook for another 10–15 minutes.
5. Adjust seasoning with salt and pepper.
6. Garnish with Parmesan cheese.

Wayne's hint ☞ This recipe is a meal by itself. Or if served as a first course, remember, don't be so generous. There's more food to come.

Escarole Fagioli with Sweet Italian Sausage

This recipe was derived from a soup called Italian Wedding (if this book is a success, you'll find it in my next book). The base of both soups is escarole, chicken stock, and garlic. Next, you can start adding some of your favorite ingredients. I like the Italian Sweet sausage and beans, but you could easily add shrimp or chicken instead of the sausage. After reading over this recipe, I feel like running to my kitchen and making this soup. My only problem is, do I add shrimp or sausage?

Serves 4–6

- 1 lb of fresh escarole, chopped
- 1 cup of onion, chopped
- 8 cups of chicken stock or 8 cups of water with 8 tsp of chicken bouillon granules
- 3/4 cup Parmesan cheese
- 2 tsp chopped garlic powder or fresh, chopped
- 2 Tbsp olive oil
- 1 lb of Sweet Italian sausage, par boiled, cooled, and cut into 1/2–inch slices
- 1–19 oz can cannelloni beans, drained (white kidney beans)

1. Sauté onions in olive oil until onions become translucent.
2. Add garlic and sauté for a few minutes, making sure garlic does not become brown.
3. Next, add chicken stock and bring to a simmer.
4. Add escarole and cook for 20–25 minutes or until escarole becomes tender.
5. Add pre-cooked sausage and the can of cannelloni beans. Allow simmering for about 5–10 minutes.
6. Sprinkle with Parmesan cheese and serve.

Wayne's hint ☞ If you can't find escarole, fresh chopped spinach works beautifully. You can also substitute rice for the white beans.

Salads

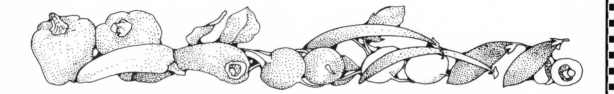

Aunt Anna's Cole Slaw (Peas and Slaw)

Great Aunt Anna, who was my Grandmother's older sister, was very special to my brothers, my sister, and me. Aunt Anna loved to cook and I especially loved this salad of hers. She always used peas, and if you like peas the way I do, this is a treat. My grandmother Helen was the second of four daughters: Anna was the eldest, Helen number two, Irene was the third, and Molly was the youngest, who played the piano for silent movies (more about her and ginger ale later). My fondest memory of the four of them together was seeing them dance the polka at a relative's wedding. These women, none of whom were over five feet tall, and all with barrel-like builds, were whirling and twirling to a German tune, dancing together as partners. To this day it brings tears of joy to my eyes. I was blessed as a child to have seen it, and even more blessed as an adult to remember it.

Serves 4–6

8 cups of green cabbage, shredded
1 cup of green peas, frozen
1 cup of mayonnaise or as needed to taste
1 Tbsp of sugar
1 Tbsp of white vinegar
Salt and pepper to taste

1. **In a large bowl, mix sugar and vinegar until sugar is dissolved.**
2. **Next, add mayonnaise.**
3. **Add peas.**
4. **Add cabbage and toss.**
5. **Adjust mayonnaise and seasonings with salt and pepper.**
6. **Chill and serve.**

Wayne's hint ☞ This salad, with its peas, is a great topper for a bar-b-que pork sandwich. Now, if you don't like the peas, take them out. It's still a good slaw and Aunt Anna's not around to know, nor do I think she would care. Can you believe all this talk about peas?

Broccoli Salad

It should be called Brokke Salad for all the times my nieces and nephews have requested this recipe when they come over or when I visit them. This dish also reminds me of Aunt Anna because, like her, I've become famous for my broccoli salad like she became famous for her peas and slaw. When I made it for one of my TV segments, NBC anchor Dave Durian commented: "you could put erasers in this dressing and they would taste good."

Serves 4–6

8 cups of broccoli, florets and chopped stems
1 cup of cheddar cheese, shredded
1 cup of red onion, sliced very thin, julienne cut
1 cup of bacon, chopped or crumbled
2 cups of mayonnaise
1/4 cup of vinegar
1/4 cup of sugar

1. **Using a whisk blend together vinegar and sugar until sugar is dissolved. Set aside.**
2. **Add mayonnaise. Blend thoroughly and set aside.**
3. **In a large bowl, toss onion, bacon, broccoli and cheese.**
4. **Add dressing and toss gently.**

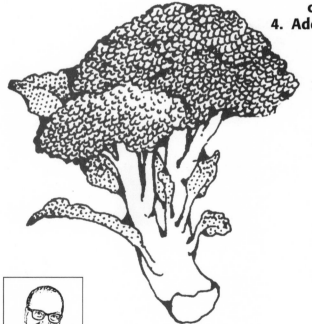

Wayne's hint ☞ Please use the stems—it adds a wonderful crunch. Broccoli should be washed, strained, and dry. Place in refrigerator for 1–2 hours for added crispness.

Carrot Salad

This is a recipe from a bygone era. It takes me back to the days when department stores in Baltimore, Hutzler's, Hochschild-Kohn, Hecht's, and Stewart's all had tearooms. With the advent of the suburbs and the way customers now shop, the tearooms disappeared (can we have a moment of silence please). One of my favorite things used to be to order at the counter of Hutzler's a shrimp salad sandwich on cheese toast with a side of carrot salad, and a large ice tea with a huge slice of lemon. It makes me happy just thinking about it.

Serves 4–6

1 lb of carrots, grated
1/2 cup of white golden raisins
1/2 cup of pineapple, chopped
1 Tbsp of sugar
1 cup of water
3/4 cup of mayonnaise or as needed to taste
Salt and pepper to taste

1. **In a pot, add water, raisins, and sugar. Simmer on low until raisins become plump.**
2. **Drain and cool raisins.**
3. **Mix mayonnaise, pineapple, raisins and carrots in a bowl.**
4. **Adjust to taste with salt and pepper.**
5. **Chill and serve.**

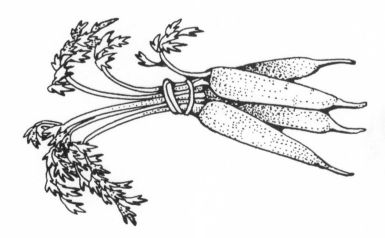

Wayne's hint ☞ The secret to the texture of this salad is making the raisins soft, which took me a long time to figure out. Can you find the secret? Email me if you can. Another plug.

Chicken Salad with Cheddar Cheese and White Grapes ⠿

Ms. Brenda, who has worked with me for more than twenty-five years at all of my restaurants, has always added 2 tsp of tarragon, fresh or dried, to this salad (behind my back, I might say—more about her later). Tarragon is one of the few herbs I do not care for. A few things I would like to say about chicken salad are: 1. I never add onions. They overpower the taste of the chicken. 2. If you feel the need for some type of onion, you should use scallions or chives, chopped very finely. 3. This recipe calls for all white meat, however the combination of white and dark meat can be used if you have leftover chicken. This salad has always been a big seller. P.S. I love Ms. Brenda.

Serves 4–6

2–2 1/2 lbs of boneless chicken breast
8 cups of water
1 cup of cheddar cheese, shredded
2 cups of celery, chopped
2 cups of white seeded grapes, cut in half
1 1/2 cups of mayonnaise or as needed
2 tsp of Dijon mustard
Salt and pepper to taste

1. **In a pot, bring water to a boil.**
2. **Add chicken and simmer for 20 minutes.**
3. **Drain chicken and cool by placing in a bowl with large amount of ice cubes. Cover with water and allow sitting for about 15 minutes or until chicken is cool. Cut into bite size cubes.**
4. **In a large bowl, blend mayonnaise and Dijon mustard.**
5. **Add cheddar cheese, celery, white grapes and cubed chicken and toss.**
6. **Adjust seasoning salt and pepper to taste.**
7. **Chill and serve.**

Wayne's hint ☞ When cooling chicken, don't let it stand too long in water and ice because it may become water logged.

P.S. It's New Year's, so I decided to try new things, starting with tarragon. I must admit, it wasn't as bad as I thought. Do I have to tell Brenda?…Nah.

Curry Chicken Salad ▪▫▪▫▪▫▪▫▪▫▪▫▪▫▪▫▪▫▪▫▪▫▪▫▪▫

Curry chicken salad brings to mind the many times I prepared it for a well-to-do couple living nearby. They had recently moved into a newly constructed, very expensive high rise on Baltimore's premiere waterfront. The building was filled mostly with empty nesters, baseball players, and numerous other celebrities. The woman's father-in-law had recently died and left them tons of money. She began to design and furnish one of the most splendid apartments in the building, combining several to accomplish the task. She had two types of gatherings to show off her new home—one for family and another for friends. The friends would get the full treatment: creative and expensive dishes, lavish deserts, and expensive wines. Conversely, at the family gatherings, the menu changed. We would sit for hours pondering what she should serve her friends. The menus for family gatherings, however, weren't extravagant in the least. Friends got shrimp, family got chicken. Once she wanted a cake for a family member's birthday. Ms. Brenda made it. I opened the box for inspection before it was delivered and realized it was only one layer. With great surprise I yelled, "Brenda it's only one layer!" Ms. Brenda responded, "That's what she wanted, she said it's only for her son-in-law."

I've got another story. This same woman wanted poached salmon—which costs hundreds of dollars—for her friends. She wanted the head and tail on. We poached the salmon and cut cucumbers very, very thinly to look like scales. It was beautiful and ready to go. Then I realized the head was missing; we had the tail but no head! So I sent Ms. Bea to the fish market to retrieve the head we had left behind. She came back and told us that some Chinese folks had bought the head that was rightfully ours. She asked them for it, but they declined. So, she went to the fishmonger and told him the story and he gave her a replacement. When the package arrived, we discovered it was from a different kind of fish. We had a salmon body with a grouper head. Have you ever seen a grouper head? It's ugly and looks like a bulldog. We laughed so hard thinking how can we serve this? When our mirth subsided, the answer was . . . garnishment. The customer was happy and the next day she called to order five pounds of curry chicken salad—for her family, of course.

Serves 4–6

2– 2 1/2 lbs of boneless chicken
  breast
3 quarts of water
2 cups of broccoli florets, poached
1 cup of red pepper, medium
  chopped
1 cup of green pepper, medium
  chopped
2 cups of red delicious apples,
  half inch cubes
1/2 cup of scallions, finely
  chopped
1/2 cup of raisins
1/2 cup of cashews
1 Tbsp of Dijon mustard
1 Tbsp of curry powder or to taste
1 tsp of garlic powder or fresh,
  chopped
1 tsp of ginger powder
1 1/2 cup of mayonnaise or as
  needed to your taste (I like
  Mayo so you may need to
  adjust.)
Salt and pepper to taste

1. In a large pot, bring water to a boil and add
   chicken. Cook for 10 to 15 minutes or until
   chicken is fully cooked.
2. Drain chicken and cool by placing in a bowl with
   large amount of ice cubes. Cover with water and
   allow sitting for about 15 minutes or until
   chicken is cooling. Don't let it stand too long
   because it may become water logged. Cut into
   bite size cubes.
3. In a large bowl mix mayonnaise, curry powder,
   ginger, mustard and garlic. Salt and pepper to
   taste.
4. Add poached chicken and toss.
5. Next, add raisins, cashews, scallions, broccoli, red
   and green peppers and apples toss.
6. Chill for at least I hour, serve over lettuce with
   sliced tomatoes.

Wayne's hint ☞ You can make your own curry powder—it's a combination of spices. Just
read the ingredients on the label of your curry powder. Pull the spices from your cupboard
and experiment. I use a coffee grinder when mixing my combination. Remember that it can
turn a container yellow.

Cucumber Salad

This salad has been a favorite in my family since I can remember. The person who makes it the best and has shown me the tricks of the salad is Laura Nantz (Willie's wife). I've changed some of the ingredients to suit my taste. But the biggest secret is the thinness of the onions and the cucumbers, which is what I learned from Laura, or as I call her Laura Lou, the pinochle-playing mother-in-law of my younger brother, Vernon. Oh, by the way, she taught my then eight-year-old nephew, Gregory how to play pinochle because she believed he's lucky. The funny thing is they usually win.

Serves 4–6

2 cups of onion, sliced very thin
4 cups of cucumber, forked and sliced very thin
2 tsp of sugar
1 cup of mayonnaise
1/4 cup of sour cream
2 Tbsp of vinegar
1 Tbsp of fresh dill, chopped fine
Salt and pepper to taste

1. **In a large bowl, dissolve sugar in the vinegar, then add sour cream and mayonnaise, and blend.**
2. **Add dill, salt and pepper.**
3. **Add onion and cucumbers, toss.**
4. **Chill and serve.**

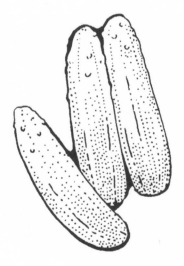

Wayne's hint ☞ More salt will tone down the bitterness of the vinegar if needed. This hint isn't just for this salad, it's for all salads when vinegar is used.

Wayne's Garbanzo Bean Salad

Serves 4–6

1–19 oz can of garbanzo beans, drained (also called chickpeas and ceci)

4 cups of tomatoes, cut into medium size wedges, then cut wedges in half (approximately 3 large tomatoes)

2 cups of cucumber, forked, quartered, seeds removed, cut into 1/2 inch slices

2 cups of green pepper, cut into 1/2 inch cubes

1 cup of onion, julienne cut

Dressing Ingredients

1/2 cup of olive oil

1/4 cup of red wine vinegar

4 anchovies, chopped (optional)

1 tsp of dill, fresh or dried

1 tsp of garlic powder or fresh, chopped

1. Place tomatoes, cucumber, green pepper and onion into a large bowl.
2. Add garbanzo beans and toss.
3. In a separate bowl, whisk together olive oil, red wine vinegar, anchovies, dill and garlic.
4. Pour dressing over salad using more or less to fit your taste. I don't always use all of the dressing.

Wayne's hint ☞ This is a great salad for adding cooked shrimp, crab meat and calamari. I think this is a wonderful combination. I used this recipe with the seafood for Christmas Eve dinner, known as The Feast of the Seven Fishes.

Greek Village Salad

When I was in my early twenties I would visit a local Greek restaurant every Friday with my friends Herschel and Sally. I had very little money, so they would always treat. I routinely ordered the Greek Salad and fried squid. When I opened my first restaurant, I recalled how wonderful that salad was and put it on the menu. It remained one of the most popular salads on our menu for years.

Serves 4–6

4 cups of tomatoes, cut into medium size wedges
2 cups of green peppers, diced into large pieces
1 cup of yellow onion, julienne cut
2 cups of cucumbers, forked, quartered, seeds removed and cubed
8 oz of feta cheese, crumbled
1 cup of Greek olives, kalamata
1/2 cup of pepperoncini
1/4 cup of fresh or dried dill, chopped

Dressing

1/2 cup of olive oil
1/4 cup of red wine vinegar
2 tsp of oregano
1 tsp of garlic powder or fresh, chopped
1 anchovy, minced, optional

1. In a serving bowl, combine tomatoes, cucumbers, onion, green peppers, Greek olives, pepperoncini and dill.
2. In a separate bowl, combine olive oil, red wine vinegar, oregano, garlic and anchovy, being sure to mix well.
3. Pour your desired amount of dressing over vegetables. You be the judge of the amount used. I don't always use all of the dressing.
4. Add Feta cheese and toss.

Wayne's hint ☞ You should serve this salad at almost room temperature so the tomatoes are not too cold. Tomatoes lose their taste if they're too cold. This used to be the favorite of the Brokke family until the broccoli salad came on the scene.

Wayne's Tomato Salad

A very good friend of mine, Carolyn Bartoli, inspired this recipe. I first met both Carolyn and her husband Dino, whom I always call Poppy, about thirty years ago, when they were both about the age I am now—fifty-three. They were born in Pennsylvania to Italian immigrants. Poppy's father's family was so large that the children were named using numbers, in Italian, one, two, three, and so on (imagine having a sister named Two!). Poppy is so full of life and fun that to this day he makes Carolyn, his wife of sixty years, chuckle with joy. For me he does the same, including turning one of my shoes into a lamp. Carolyn always remarked that this was a summertime salad. So, wait for the best, ripest Maryland tomatoes July through October. A question I'm always asked is why I don't use vinegar. The answer is, the tomatoes have enough acidity. I enjoy a big slice of crusty bread to dip into the sauce that is created by this wonderful dressing and fresh, ripe, Maryland tomatoes.

Serves 4–6

4 cups of ripe tomatoes, cubed
1 Tbsp of garlic powder or fresh, chopped
1 cup of onion, julienne cut, thinly sliced
1/3 cup of extra virgin olive oil
10 large leaves of fresh basil, thinly sliced

1. **In a large serving bowl, mix tomatoes, garlic, onion, and basil.**
2. **Add the olive oil.**
3. **Salt and pepper to taste.**
4. **Allow to sit at room temperature for 20 minutes before serving.**

Wayne's hint ☞ You should always use the best olive oil for this salad. A trick with the garlic is to leave it whole and place a toothpick in it. After the salad has set for a bit, take the toothpick with the garlic out. This is a way to get the garlic flavor without the bitterness.

Aunt Mae's Macaroni Salad with Tuna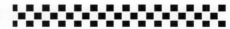

I love the use of tuna in this salad. My Aunt Mae made it that way and it brings back many memories, including of her family, whom I always thought were rather humorous. Her name was Maitresse Chester. Her father wanted a boy, so he named her Chester. Her mother's name was Blanche and she made wonderful chicken and dumplings. She always kept Chihuahuas. In fact, one day, one of her Chihuahuas was sitting on Aunt Mae's nine-month pregnant tummy when the baby gave a kick that sent the dog flying across the room! Mae's grandmother had one of the best names I've ever heard in my life: Evangeline Clementine Lucinda Eveline. I could never remember her last name because she had too many first names and I was only ten years old. I do remember when I went to Culpeper, VA where Evangeline lived out her life. In the graveyard where she was buried there were a lot of rhyming names on the tombstones. Imagine a place where the parents rhymed their children's names—what a sweet tradition. Thanks Auntie Mae, love ya!

Serves 4–6

1 lb of elbow macaroni
1/2 cup of celery, chopped
1/2 cup of scallions, thinly sliced
   using the green and white
1/2 cup of green pepper, chopped
1/2 cup of red pepper, chopped
1/2 cup of carrot, grated
1 1/2 cups of mayonnaise or as
   needed
1–6 1/8 oz can of tuna solid white
   in water, drained and flaked
2 Tbsp of sugar
2 Tbsp of white vinegar
Salt and pepper to taste

1. Cook macaroni, drain and cool.
2. In a large bowl, mix mayonnaise, vinegar, sugar,
   salt and pepper
3. Next add carrots, celery, scallions, red and green
   peppers.
4. Add tuna.
5. Add cooled macaroni and toss.
6. Chill and serve.

Wayne's hint ☞ When tuna isn't on sale and shrimp is, you can use shrimp in this recipe.

Italian Mixed Salad

This salad was created for my love of Italian food—especially antipasto. Ms. Bea has become famous for making it. Twenty-five years ago, her son was working for me as a dishwasher and every night he would leave before his shift was over. At the end of the week I let him go. The next day, Ms. Bea showed up to apologize for her son's poor behavior. I wasn't interested in her apology because I was too busy and she could tell. She asked me what she could do to make up for it. I told her she could wash dishes, and she did. The rest is history. Ms. Bea still works with me to this day. She is the most special person a restaurateur could ever wish for—an angel sent from restaurant heaven who has never missed a day in more than twenty years—a record even for Cal Ripken, Jr. I'm not the only one who loves Ms. Bea—everyone does.

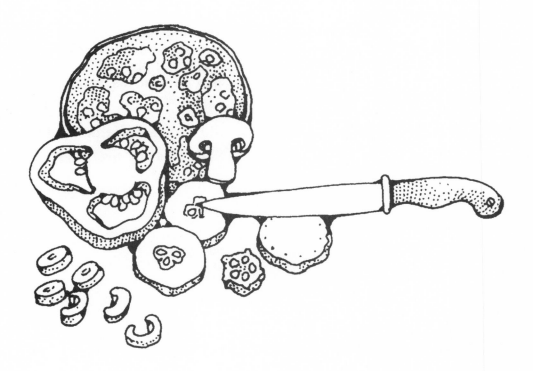

Serves 4–6

2 cups of Genoa salami, bite size
1 cup of green peppers, cubed
1 cup of red sweet peppers, cubed
4 cups of tomatoes, wedged
1 cup of onion, julienne
2 cups of cucumbers, forked, quartered, seeds removed, and cut into 1/2 inch slices
1 cup of black pitted olives, whole
1 cup of whole green Spanish olives (pimento)
2 cups of provolone cheese, bite size
1/2 cup of olive oil
1/4 cup of red wine vinegar
1 Tbsp of oregano
1 tsp of garlic powder or fresh, chopped fine
2 Tbsp of anchovies, chopped fine (optional)
Salt and pepper to taste

Salad

1. In a large salad bowl, place green and red peppers, tomatoes, onions, and cucumbers.
2. Next, add provolone cubes, black and green olives and salami.
3. Mix dressing.
4. Pour dressing over salad.
5. Toss and serve.

Dressing

6. In a medium bowl, whisk together olive oil, vinegar, oregano, garlic, and anchovies.
7. Adjust seasoning with salt and pepper.
8. Drizzle over salad using more or less to fit your taste and serve.

Wayne's hint ☞ I think it's important to use the best salami and provolone. It will make all the difference in the taste of your salad.

Wayne's Couscous Salad

Couscous is usually found in Mediterranean and Middle Eastern dishes. I have prepared this recipe at my restaurants and at home for many years. I love to serve this is on a platter (while it's still hot), topped with grilled chicken and shrimp.

Serves 4–6

2 cups of water
1 tsp of olive oil
1 cup of celery, chopped fine
1 cup of carrots, chopped fine
1 cup of scallions, chopped fine
1 loose cup of golden raisins
1–10 oz box of couscous

Dressing
1/3 cup of olive oil
1 Tbsp of garlic powder or fresh, chopped
Salt and pepper to taste

1. Add 1 tsp of olive oil and a dash of salt to water and bring to a boil.
2. Add couscous.
3. Remove from heat, cover and let sit for 5 minutes (stir once with a fork to break up lumps)
4. Toss in vegetables and raisins.
5. In a separate bowl mix together dressing ingredients (olive oil, garlic and salt and pepper) and then mix into couscous.
6. Serve warm or chill and then serve.

Wayne's hint ☞ You can also chill this dish and serve it as a cold side salad. Couscous is really a pasta. Could you imagine making pasta that small?

The Best Shrimp Salad Ever ▪■▪■▪■▪■▪■▪■▪■▪■▪■

I grew up in Sparrows Point (called the Point), a steel mill area near Baltimore. There were six churches, streets that went East-West alphabetically A to J, and North-South numerically 200–1100. I lived in the 1000 block of H. The house number was 1007 H Street. We had the first kindergarten in the state of Maryland, an elementary school, a junior high school, and a high school. There was a company store, a bowling alley, restaurants, grocery stores, and a gas station. The only thing this town of nearly 5,000 residents did not have was a bar. Liquor was never sold on the Point. Now, on your way into the Point the road was overcrowded with liquor stores and beer joints. There was one place that sold great food, liquor, *and* you could cash your paycheck. This recipe was inspired by the best shrimp salad sandwiches I have ever eaten—at Mickey's, a beer joint just outside Sparrows Point where you could cash checks, buy liquor, and eat great food. What more could you ask for?

Serves 4–6

3 lbs of shrimp
1 cup of celery, diced
1 cup of mayonnaise, or as needed (Some people like a little, I like to use a lot.)
1/4 cup of vinegar
1 cup of water
1 Tbsp of Old Bay ® seasoning or Cajun spices (Please try to get the Old Bay ® seasoning. If you like this salad to be spicier just add more of the seasoning.)
1 1/2 cups of large Spanish olives with pimentos, cut in half

1. **With shells on, steam shrimp in vinegar, water, and Old Bay ® or Cajun spice (you can use 1/2 cup of water and 1/2 cup of beer in place of 1 cup of water.**
2. **Cool shrimp quickly with ice, strain, peel, de-vein and allow to dry.**
3. **Mix the mayonnaise and seasoning thoroughly.**
4. **Toss together the olives, celery and shrimp.**
5. **Add seasoned mayonnaise and mix.**
6. **Adjust seasoning and if you need more mayonnaise, do so.**

Wayne's hint ☞ Please use large shrimp, for example U10, U12, U15—the number represents the quantity of shrimp per pound. The secret is the size of the shrimp. The larger the better.

Original Pasta Salad

Several people from church catered my sister Patricia's wedding. To my delight, the one dish she requested from me was this pasta salad. Her wedding was scheduled for early evening and she asked if I would be one of the ushers. She was very understanding when I told her that Saturday nights were very busy and I couldn't take off. She changed the time of her wedding so I could attend.

I ran two restaurants and worked seven days a week, ten to sixteen hours a day. Sometimes I would have to take a nap on the second floor in order to work the night. One day I realized, "I'm fifty . . . my God, how could this have happened? Could I do this all again? I wasn't paying attention!" I told this story to Ms. Brenda and her sister Anna. They laughed and said, "You *were* paying attention. You were just running back and forth between two restaurants and the time passed. . . ."

As one grateful brother to his sister who changed her wedding plans for me, now I wish I had paid more attention. When you know better, you do better.

Serves 4–6

1 lb of pasta
1 cup of red pepper, chopped
2 cups of broccoli, florets
1/2 pint of cherry tomatoes, cut into halves
2 cups of zucchini, quartered and sliced thin
1 cup of black olives, small, whole
3/4 cup of pine nuts
1 cup of olive oil, or to taste
1/4 cup of Parmesan cheese, grated
1 Tbsp of garlic powder or fresh, chopped
2 Tbsp of fresh basil or 2 tsp of dried
Salt and pepper to taste

1. Cook pasta for 15 minutes. Drain and cool.
2. In a saucepan, sauté pine nuts in olive oil until golden brown.
3. When pine nuts are golden remove from heat and cool.
4. In a large bowl, place pasta, broccoli, red pepper, black olives, tomatoes, zucchini, basil and garlic and toss.
5. Add Parmesan cheese.
6. Pour pine nuts and oil over pasta and vegetables, toss.
7. Salt and pepper to taste.
8. You may serve at this point or chill.

Wayne's hint ☞ Sorry, no other nut will do, so please find pine nuts. The tri-color pasta shells or corkscrews look great and they will hold the dressing better than flat pasta.

Lady H's Potato Salad ▪▫▪▫▪▫▪▫▪▫▪▫▪▫▪▫▪▫▪▫▪▫▪▫▪

If you have read the beginning of this cookbook, you know why there are pickles in this recipe. There's more to this recipe. It has to do with the olives.

They come from a regular customer who lived in the neighborhood a long time ago. Her much older husband had recently died. I think he was about seventy and she was around thirty-five. She was lonely and had plenty of time on her hands . . . and a lot of money. So, she ate at my restaurant twice a day. She was a nice, kind lady who adopted our staff and me for companionship. I was around twenty-eight at the time. I don't know if adoption is the right word when it came to me— her interest seemed far greater than the usual restaurant groupie. Need I say more? Gifts and business expansion were offered, but at a price more than friendship. She pursued and I ran. To my surprise, the lady in question (that hussy) was invited by the staff to our first Christmas party. I was disappointed but polite. It was a potluck party and Lady H brought potato salad with olives. The dish was inspiring even if she wasn't. Well, she finally got the hint. Six months later she married someone nearly half her age. Six months after that she died and left him all her money. What a crazy thing: he got the money and I got the salad. Somehow, I think it's fair.

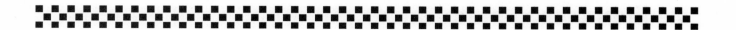

Serves 6

2 1/2 lbs of red potatoes, cubed,
  skin on
1 cup of scallions, thinly sliced
  using the white and green parts
4 hard boiled eggs, chopped
2 cups of mayonnaise, more or
  less to taste
1 Tbsp of mustard, Dijon or yellow
  (I like Dijon in this recipe.)
1/2 cup of pickles, chopped
1 Tbsp of pickle juice
1/2 cup of green olives, sliced
Salt and pepper to taste

1. Place potatoes in a pot and cover with cold water. Allow to simmer (not boil) until potatoes can be easily pierced with a fork.
2. Drain and cool the potatoes.
3. In a large bowl, combine mayonnaise, mustard, eggs, pickle juice and scallions.
4. Add pickles and olives.
5. Now add the cool potatoes and toss.
6. Salt and pepper to taste.
7. Chill for at least 1–2 hours.
8. Garnish with paprika.

Wayne's hint ☞ What I would like to tell you about this recipe is that if you decide not to use the pickles, try a tablespoon of pickle juice. It makes the mayonnaise smooth, silky, and creamy.

Mediterranean Potato Salad

This recipe was created in the summer of 2001. A good friend, Dean (whom I've known since he was seven years old and is now thirty-seven), and I were contemplating going on a vacation with some other friends. Cuba was one of the destinations and the Amalfi Coast of Italy was the other. By coincidence, the next day in *The New York Times* travel section there was a large article on Amalfi and its cuisine. All the recipes in the article used fresh ingredients, including a variety of fish and vegetables of bountiful summertime. With a little from this and a little from that, the recipe was born.

Serves 4–6

4 cups of red potatoes, skin on
2 cups of tomatoes, cubed
1 1/2 cups of white onions, julienne cut
1 cup of black olives, pitted, medium size (When it comes to olives, the recipe can be changed to incorporate your favorites.)
1 cup of Spanish olives, medium size
2 Tbsp of capers
1/4 cup of fresh basil, thinly sliced (If you don't have fresh Basil don't do the recipe.)
Olive oil as needed
Salt and pepper to taste

1. **Boil red potatoes until they are fork tender. Drain and allow to cool. Refrigerate until cold.**
2. **Once cold, cut into 1/4 slices. Add tomatoes, onions, olives, and capers. Gently toss.**
3. **Next, drizzle olive oil over mixture, to your taste.**
4. **Season with salt and pepper and add basil.**
5. **Toss gently and serve.**

Wayne's hint ☞ You can add tuna to this recipe and call it a Mediterranean Nicoise. Another variation would be to add shrimp or serve it as a main dish.

Tom's Grilled Chicken Salad

The year Bugs Bunny turned fifty, Mickey Mouse was sixty and my father turned seventy, was the year this salad was created. A friend of mine, Tom, was also turning fifty. I prepared lunch for him and his family. There were fifty multi-colored helium balloons and glasses from a local gas station depicting Bugs Bunny's fiftieth birthday. This made for a festive occasion.

The centerpiece of this meal was, as I called it, Tom's Grilled Chicken Salad. I had started grilling chicken for lunch. Then, I was stumped about the rest of the menu. Looking in my cupboard for inspiration, I discovered I had cans of black olives and several cans of mandarin oranges (which were kept for my niece Karren, since that was the only fruit she would eat). With that, I thought, let's just chop the chicken and make a salad.

Serves 4–6

2 1/2–3 lbs chicken breasts, boneless
2 Tbsp of rosemary, fresh
1–16 oz can of black olives, pitted
2 cups of chopped walnuts
2 cups of celery, chopped
1/2 cup of olive oil for dressing (You will also need just enough olive oil to brush your chicken with before grilling.)
Enough olive oil to brush chicken
1 tsp of garlic powder or fresh, chopped
1–11 oz can of mandarin oranges
Salt and pepper to taste

1. **Brush chicken with olive oil and grill until done.**
2. **Cut chicken into bite-size cubes.**
3. **In a bowl, place chicken, olives, walnuts and celery.**
4. **Add olive oil, garlic and rosemary. Toss.**
5. **Adjust seasoning using salt and pepper.**
6. **Top with mandarin oranges.**
7. **Chill and serve.**

Wayne's hint ☞ Always remember to toss the salad first and then top with mandarin oranges so that they don't break apart.

Red Beet Salad with Walnuts and Red Grapes ▨▨▨▨▨▨

I happen to love red beets. Until recently, the only recipes I have that use them are pickled beets with pickled eggs and borscht. Not many people like beets. In fact, Dave Durian, a newscaster for WBAL, NBC's Baltimore affiliate, once said to me, "If you don't ever feel like feeding the staff at the station, just bring pickled beets and pickled eggs—you'll have no takers." Yvette tells me that her Grandmother Irene (should I sing the song now?) would love me because *she* loves beets. I say, red beet lovers of the world unite! Sorry, back to the salad. In my search for something new to do with beets I came across a salad at the newly renovated Grand Central Station in New York. The Grand Central Market, once a loading dock, was recently completed by Michael Ewing (I'll also mention Charlie Johnson because I like him and he works for Michael), the man who gave me my first lease at Harborplace at Baltimore's Inner Harbor. It is there that I found my inspiration for this salad. The red grapes complement the sweetness of the beets and the nuts add a wonderful crunchiness. The sour cream and goat cheese add a hint of a savory borscht.

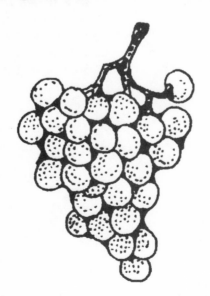

Serves 4

4–14 1/2 oz cans of sliced or
  medium sized whole, quartered
  red beets, drained, not pickled
  or sweetened or 6 cups of fresh
  cooked red beets (fork tender)
1 cup of walnuts
2 cups of red seedless grapes, cut
  in half
1/4 cup of red wine vinegar
1/2 cup of extra virgin olive oil
Salt and Pepper to taste

1. Cut red beets into 1/2 inch julienne slices and
   place in large salad bowl.
2. Add walnuts and grapes and gently toss.
3. In a separate bowl, whip together vinegar and oil,
   salt and pepper.
4. Pour the mixture over top of the red beets,
   walnuts, and grapes.
5. Adjust seasoning using salt and pepper.
6. Serve cold garnished with goat cheese or sour
   cream and chives.

Wayne's hint ☞ You can use fresh beets. If I have the time, that's what I do. Since I seldom have the time, I use canned.

Holiday Turkey and Ham Salad :::::::::::::::::::::::::::

At both my mother and grandmother's houses, holiday meals always included ham, turkey, and roast beef. It really didn't matter if it was Christmas, Thanksgiving, or Easter—it was like the Holy trinity. I think it was mostly to insure that there were lots of leftovers to take home, rather than to satisfy a variety of tastes. I continued this tradition until I realized I didn't have to, but by then I was approaching forty. I still laugh about the way the leftovers were divvied up. The matriarchy would control this very carefully, making each of us a doggie bag. But my allotment always seemed to be minus the roast beef. How could that be? Did they love my older brother more? Were they saving it for the mailman, or maybe their priest? To this day it remains a mystery. Since I never got any of the beef, I created my own tradition with this wonderful turkey and ham salad—without the tarragon of course. This salad is perfect for holiday leftovers.

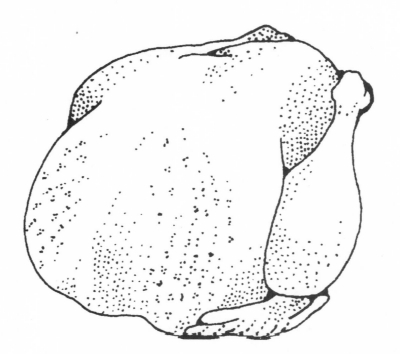

Serves 4–6

4 cups of turkey, cubed
1 cup of ham, cubed
1 cup of cheddar cheese, shredded
2 cups of celery, chopped
1 1/2 cups of mayonnaise, or as
needed
1 Tbsp Dijon mustard
1 tsp of tarragon (optional, but
Ms. Brenda would add it.)
Salt and pepper to taste

1. **In a large bowl, mix mayonnaise, Dijon mustard, tarragon, salt and pepper.**
2. **Next, add cheese, celery, and toss.**
3. **Add turkey and ham, toss.**
4. **Adjust seasoning with salt and pepper.**
5. **Chill and serve.**

Wayne's hint ☞ This is a great recipe to use with leftover roast beef. That is, of course, if you're the one that got the beef.

Seafood Tortellini

If you ask Ms. Brenda, Ms. Anna, Ms. Bea, or me—all of us have worked together for more than twenty-five years—what our favorite salad is, we would all answer in unison: "Seafood Tortellini, the kind with large tortellini, the size of a silver dollar." The creaminess of the dressing, the size of the shrimp, and the size of the tortellini make for such a wonderful blend of textures and tastes.

This salad became the favorite of a local bail bondsman and his cronies. He would arrive in a large silver Mercedes Benz, and every accessory that should have been made of chrome, including the bumper, was gold. All four doors would open at once and four or five large, well-dressed men with alligator shoes and gold chains and rings would strut into the restaurant. There behind the counter would be Brenda, Anna, and Bea—what a hoot. Once we got to know them they were as gentle and kind as could be. They had a story they never told—and we never asked. After buying fifty or a hundred dollars worth of tortellini salad, they would sometimes tip the ladies another hundred. They were regulars. They came in two or three times a month, exit the same way they arrived, and drive off.

Serves 4–6

1 lb of shrimp (U12 or U15, this
   refers to the number of shrimp
   per pound)
1 lb of spinach tortellini, cooked
   and cooled (cool by placing
   tortellini on a tray, spread out,
   and putting in refrigerator until
   you reach step number seven.)
1/2 lb of crabmeat, back fin
6 cups of water
1–8 oz can of sliced water
   chestnuts, drained
4 oz of pimentos, julienne sliced
1/4 cup of ketchup
1/4 cup of white wine
1 cup of mayonnaise
Salt and pepper to taste

1. **In a pot, bring water to a boil, drop in shrimp with
   shells on. Cook for 10 minutes.**
2. **Place shrimp in a large bowl and cover with ice.
   Then cover with water. Let it sit for about 5
   minutes. Remove shrimp from ice and water.**
3. **Peel and de-vein shrimp.**
4. **In a bowl, place shrimp, crabmeat, water chestnuts
   and pimentos.**
5. **In a separate bowl, mix mayonnaise, ketchup and
   white wine.**
6. **Next, pour over seafood mixture.**
7. **Salt and pepper to taste.**
8. **Add tortellini, toss, chill and serve.**

Wayne's hint ☞ It's important to add the pasta at the end because tossing too much
could cause it to break apart.

Turkey Waldorf Salad

Once upon a time there was a producer for NBC's Baltimore affiliate, WBAL. He called and begged me to do the Thanksgiving Day show. The problem with the request was that it was the day before Thanksgiving. I said to him, "I need more lead time to prepare a recipe and assemble the ingredients." He begged and he begged and he begged. It was pitiful. So, I told him I'd think about it and call him back. I thought about what I could put together on such short notice—while I was preparing my Thanksgiving Day meal. You have to understand that I was actually invited to a friend's for Thanksgiving that year, but I didn't trust that they would share their leftovers—most people don't. I've been stung so many times, I always make a complete turkey dinner with all the fixings regardless. I believe that on Thanksgiving one should eat two or three times! Could you imagine not being able to have a piece of pumpkin pie later that night? So, as it turns out, his begging worked. I gave him some of my turkey, but I didn't share any of the fixings. This salad was created for his show. Five days later he was fired. He got the boot and I got the recipe!

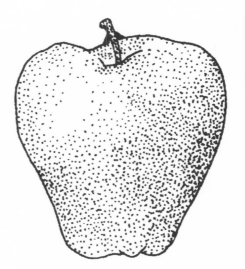

Serves 4

4 cups of turkey, cubed
2 cups of celery, sliced
1 red apple, unpeeled, cored and
  cubed
1 cup of cheddar cheese, shredded
1/2–1 cup golden white raisins
1/2–1 cup walnut, toasted
1 1/2 cups of mayonnaise or as
  needed
Salt and pepper to taste

1. In a large bowl, mix mayonnaise, cheese, raisins
   and walnuts.
2. Add apple and celery, toss.
3. Next, add turkey and toss again.
4. Adjust seasoning using salt and pepper.
5. Chill and serve.

Wayne's hint ☞ Place walnuts in toaster oven or regular oven for 10 minutes. This will bring out the flavor of the nut. It wakes up the nut and brings out its oil—AKA flavor.

Watercress Salad

This is one of the salads I've been making since before my days as a restaurateur. I was living at the time in a dollar house. Yes, I said a *dollar*.

I know that sounds strange. It was 1976. Baltimore was in the process of developing its Inner Harbor and adjacent neighborhoods. Abandoned buildings were removed from the waterfront and a beautiful brick promenade took their place.

The neighborhood adjoining the harbor was known as the Otterbeine, a name taken from the church that dominates the area. At the time, the houses in this area were condemned and marked for demolition. A historian for the city pointed out how important the homes and other structures were to the city's heritage. The houses dated as far back as the late 1700s. The city decided to promote homesteading in the area. If you were capable financially of renovating one of the homes, the city would sell it to you for one dollar. Sounded good to me.

So, I applied for 113 West Hill Street—not too big and not too small—just right. Well, twenty-three other people thought the same thing. Because there was such a demand, there ended up being a lottery. Names were picked from a large bowl for each house being sold. When it came time for 113 West Hill Street, the number of people was reduced to two, which caused me great concern. There was one winner and one loser. But when the name was pulled from the bowl, it was mine. I was twenty-six years old and had just quit my job at Hess Shoe Store. I had no idea how I would pay for the renovations.

Still, it was a glorious night. The sky was clear and the temperature was in the low seventies. As I walked from the church with my friend Senie toward the promenade, there was a tall ship docked and the Baltimore Symphony was playing. I was filled with such excitement and joy for the future of the city. But inside I was worried how I would pay for the renovations. Well, I did it—somehow. When my house was completed I served this salad many times.

At that time there was no casual restaurant in Baltimore. My friends who loved my cooking encouraged me to open a restaurant where you could get simple yet delicious meals like soups, salads, and

Serves 4–6

1 lb of watercress, washed and
  drained
2 granny smith apples, cored and
  wedged
4 oz of blue cheese
2/3 cup of olive oil
1/3 cup of red wine vinegar
1 cup of walnuts, whole pieces,
  toasted
Salt and pepper to taste (Salt
  takes away the tartness of the
  vinegar.)

1. Wash and drain watercress.
2. Place on a serving plate.
3. Next, top with crumbled blue cheese and sprinkle with
     walnuts.
4. Place apple slices around greens.
5. Whisk together olive oil and red wine vinegar.
6. Adjust seasoning with salt and pepper.
7. Sprinkle dressing over salad using more or less to your
     taste and serve.

Wayne's hint ☞ This recipe calls for 1 pound of watercress, which sounds like a lot. Pick some of the stem off, which reduces the amount significantly. Sometimes, I use just the leaves.

Apple Walnut Tuna Salad :▪:▪:▪:▪:▪::▪::▪:▪::▪:▪:

I created this recipe for The Soup Kitchen, Ltd. When I first opened this restaurant we only served soups, salads, and desserts. The menu expanded in time to include sandwiches and light entrees. One of the first sandwiches to debut was a Tuna, Cucumber, and Swiss Cheese on an Italian roll. Then came the Tuna Melt. Remember those? Where's Margaret Mead when you need her? Anyway, as trends will come and go so did the tuna melt. Its main ingredient was tuna salad and that was definitely not trendy. So, this recipe for a basic tuna salad has remained through many incarnations and is still on the menu today in the form of a Tuna Sandwich (novel idea, huh?).

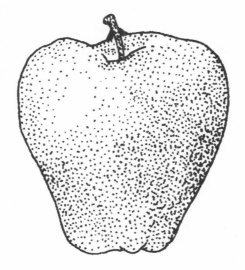

Serves 4

2–6 1/8 oz cans solid white tuna
   in water
1 cup of celery, chopped
1 cup of onion, chopped
1/2 red apple, cored and chopped
1/2 cup of walnut, toasted and
   chopped
1/4 cup of mayonnaise, more or
   less to taste
Salt and pepper to taste

1. Drain tuna.
2. In a bowl, flake tuna.
3. Add celery, onion, walnuts and apple, toss.
4. Fold in mayonnaise.
5. Salt and pepper to taste.

Wayne's hint ☞ I always keep my tuna fish in the refrigerator because I think it's healthier, and when I want to make a tuna salad, it's cold and ready to go.

Entrees

Wayne's Beef Macaroni and Cheese ▰▱▰▱▰▱▰▱▰▱▰▱

Every Friday I do a three-minute cooking segment on NBC's local affiliate, WBAL. I have been doing this for more than eight years. Not only do I prepare a recipe for the TV audience, but I also make enough to feed most of the staff. On some Fridays I feed as many as thirty or forty people, almost everyone at the station. Apart from my ribs, macaroni and cheese is perhaps the staff's favorite—they could eat it every week. Whenever there's a special occasion such as a birthday, retirement, or maternity leave, I will offer to feature this dish for the viewers *and* for them. I can't prepare it on the show as often as they would like, so I'm always looking to develop new recipes using this dish. This is one of those recipes. There's also Broccoli Mac and Cheese, Italian Sausage Mac and Cheese, and Ham and Asparagus Mac and Cheese. I've been challenged to come up with these creations so: 1. Viewers out there in TV land get a new version each time and 2. the staff get to indulge their love of macaroni and cheese.

Serves 4–6

2 lbs of lean ground beef
2 cups of white onions, chopped
2 cups of green peppers, chopped
1–28 oz can of crushed tomatoes
1 Tbsp of garlic powder or fresh,
   chopped
1–16 oz box of elbow macaroni
2–3 cups of grated cheddar cheese
1 Tbsp of basil
1 Tbsp of cumin
1 Tbsp of oregano
Olive oil as needed
Salt and pepper to taste

1. Boil macaroni noodles, drain and set aside.
2. In a pan, sauté green peppers, onions and garlic in olive oil until soft.
3. Add ground beef and sauté until brown. Drain excess fat.
4. Add crushed tomatoes, basil, cumin, oregano, salt and pepper.
5. In a large bowl, combine macaroni and beef mixture.
6. Place mixture in a 9x13 greased baking dish.
7. Top with grated cheese and bake at 350 for 20 to 25 minutes.

Wayne's hint ☞ I like the combination of spices here. If you use more cumin, you will get more of a southwestern flavor. It's the same spice that makes chili wonderful.

Chicken Cacciatore ▪▫▪▫▪▫▪▫▪▫▪▫▪▫▪▫▪▫▪▫▪▫▪▫

For years, Mr. Eddie worked around my house building decks, sidewalks, piers, and fences. One year, at Easter, he purchased a duckling for his children. By autumn, the duck was no longer yellow or small. He was white and tall and had outgrown its surroundings. I live on the water, so Mr. Eddie brought over his duck to set him free in the cove next to my house. The white duck immediately made friends with a mallard and went on his way. He wasn't seen until the following spring when Gregory opened my front door, turned and yelled for me saying, "Mr. Eddie's duck is here!" Turning back to the duck, Gregory added, "Mr. Eddie's not here." The duck paid him no mind and proceeded to camp out for several days. Whenever Gregory or I opened the front door we would tell the duck, "Mr. Eddie's not here." Finally, he was gone. Just as the swallows return to San Juan Capistrano, the Duck continues to come back to my front door every spring to wait for Mr. Eddie. It's been four years now. You may be wondering what this has to do with this recipe. Well, Mr. Eddie over the years has had only one request—always for the same recipe—chicken cacciatore. I'm so glad he didn't want duck cacciatore. I love serving this with polenta, pasta, or basil mashed potatoes.

Serves 4–6

3–4 lbs of chicken, cut into serving
  pieces
1–28 oz can of whole tomatoes,
  hand crushed
1 cup of green pepper, cubed
1 cup of red pepper, cubed
1 cup of onion, chopped
8 oz of mushrooms, thickly sliced
2 tsp of sugar
1/3 cup of olive oil or as needed
1 Tbsp of garlic powder or fresh,
  chopped
1 tsp of rosemary
1 tsp of basil
1 tsp of thyme
1 bay leaf
1/2 tsp of crushed red pepper
1/4 cup of Parmesan cheese

For Dredging
1 cup of flour
1 tsp of garlic powder or fresh,
  chopped
2 tsp of salt
2 tsp of pepper

1. Mix together flour, garlic powder, salt and pepper (items for dredging). Set aside.
2. Rinse chicken in salt water.
3. Then, dredge in flour mixture.
4. Sauté chicken pieces in oil until brown.
5. Next, remove chicken from pan, temporarily.
6. Pour off excess oil, leaving approximately 2 Tbsp.
7. Add tomatoes, peppers, onions, sugar and spices.
8. Place chicken back into pan and simmer for a about 1 hour, stirring occasionally.
9. Add mushrooms the last 10 minutes.
10. Place on a serving platter and top with Parmesan cheese.

Wayne's hint ☞ You can use breast of chicken here, though my favorite pieces are the legs and the thighs. I think they have more flavor.

Baked Ham with Pineapple Glaze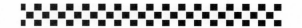

This recipe has been in my family for generations. When we know it's on the menu we anticipate the aroma that is created by the blend of pineapple, brown sugar, and spices. The presentation itself brings back warm memories. My sister-in-law Brenda, in her first year of marriage, volunteered to make the Easter ham. We arrived to a kitchen filled with that wonderful aroma. As we gazed upon the ham, it brought tears to our eyes because it looked just like Mom's and Grandmom's. We then went to the front room for conversation and appetizers. Brenda called to us when dinner was ready. Once we all were seated, she placed the ham in the center of the table. There was a huge gasp. We were all stunned to see a naked ham—no pineapple, no cherries, no glaze. Keith, her husband, asked, "What happened to the ham?" She replied, "I put it in the sink and washed everything off." We were horrified and everyone began giving her instructions on the right way the ham should have been presented. To this day, more than twenty-five years later, she still denies this story. And I continue to laugh.

Serves 4–6

1 of your favorite ham,
  approximately 6–8 lbs
1–14 oz can of pineapple rings
  (save juice for glaze)
1 small jar of maraschino cherries
10–15 whole cloves
Ham Glaze
1 cup of brown sugar, packed
  (light or dark), add more for a
  sweet tooth.
1 cup of pineapple juice (use juice
  from can)
1 Tbsp of Worcestershire Sauce
1 tsp of dry mustard
2 Tbsp of yellow mustard, please
  not Dijon

Making the Glaze
1. Mix pineapple juice and brown sugar until sugar
   dissolves.
2. Add Worcestershire sauce and dry mustard.
3. Whisk in yellow mustard.
4. Set aside.

Making the baking ham
5. Score the ham 1/2 inch deep in a crisscross
   manner.
6. Place whole cloves in scoring about 2 inches apart.
7. Next put plenty of pineapple rings all over ham.
   Secure with toothpicks.
8. In the middle of the pineapple ring place a
   maraschino cherry.
9. Spoon the pineapple glaze over ham. Cover ham
   with tented aluminum foil.
10. Bake at 325 for 20 minutes per pound. Removing
    for the last 20 minutes of baking.

Wayne's hint ☞ Always remember to let the ham rest for about 20 minutes so that when you cut into it all the juices will not run out. Your ham will become dry if you carve it too soon.

Wayne's Buffalo Wings

I believe football and chicken wings go together like baseball and hotdogs. We serve them by the bucketful at Wayne's Bar-B-Que, and at home, by the platter, garnished with scallion and cilantro. When New York and Texas opposed each other in a recent Super Bowl, I titled my TV segment "Buffalo Wings Texas Style." This made for a lot of fun. The act of eating Buffalo wings is a great equalizer among people—we are all one when it comes to food like Buffalo wings.

Serves 4–6

5 lbs of whole chicken wings
1/2 cup of onion, chopped fine
1 cup of scallions, sliced
4 oz of butter, 1 stick
1 cup of Tabasco sauce
1 Tbsp of cilantro

1. **Rinse wings in salt water. Place on baking sheet and bake at 350 for 25 minutes or until golden brown.**
2. **On medium heat, sauté onions in butter until they become translucent.**
3. **Next, add Tabasco sauce and simmer for 5 minutes.**
4. **Pour sauce over wings in a large mixing bowl.**
5. **Toss like a salad.**
6. **Place wings on large platter and garnish with scallions and cilantro.**

Wayne's hint ☞ I think it's important to rinse the wings with salt water because it helps to wash away any impurities and to tenderize the meat.

Cajun Wings

Serves 4–6

Wings are a favorite dish during Sunday football on TV. Try this one on Super Sunday.

5 lbs of whole chicken wings
1/4 lb of butter, one stick
1 cup of Tabasco sauce
1 cup of scallions, sliced
1 Tbsp of Cajun spices

1. Wash wings in salt water. Place on baking sheet and bake at 350 for 25 minutes or until golden brown.
2. Sauté onions in butter until they become translucent.
3. Next, add Tabasco sauce and Cajun spices, simmer for 5 minutes.
4. Pour sauce over wings in a large mixing bowl.
5. Toss like a salad.
6. Place wings on a large platter and garnish with scallions.

Wayne's Pulled BBQ Chicken, Pork, or Beef

When I grew up, BBQ for a Marylander was ground beef and BBQ sauce—almost a sloppy Joe. When the Orioles moved to Camden Yards, I decided to open a BBQ restaurant, so I went up and down the East Coast looking at BBQ establishments. Of all the places I researched, the one that inspired me the most was John Wayne's BBQ in Lexington, North Carolina. The owner's name was John Wayne and he must have had 500 pictures of John Wayne in his restaurant. He believes Lexington, NC is the capital of BBQ, and after eating there I would have to agree. He said two things you need to remember: 1. You slow roast your pork and you hand pull it. 2. You can bake it, roast it, boil it, or grill it, but the most important thing is the sauce. With those words of wisdom, I created what I consider to be the best BBQ sandwich on the East Coast. I have a wonderful sauce I have been using for years made with raspberry preserves for sweetness—no artificial smoke flavor and not too vinegary. Lexington might be the BBQ capital, but Wayne's Bar-B-Que in Baltimore is the White House.

Serves 4–6

3 lbs of roasted chicken, skinned
   and pulled (Try the pork and
   beef. They work great also.)
2 cups of Wayne's® BBQ sauce or
   add 2 Tbsp raspberry preserves
   to your sauce
2 cups of onion, diced
1/3 cup of white vinegar
4 oz of margarine, 1 stick

1. **In a bowl, combine the BBQ sauce and vinegar. Set
   aside.**
2. **In a large skillet, sauté onions in margarine until
   they become translucent.**
3. **Add the pulled chicken to the onions and continue
   to sauté for about 10 minutes.**
4. **Add BBQ sauce mix to chicken and onions and
   allow simmering for 20 minutes.**

Wayne's hint ☞ You can serve this with potato salad and coleslaw. Check out Aunt Anna's
Peas and Slaw (page 28) and Lady H's Potato Salad recipes (page 46).

Chicken Alison

I created this recipe when my niece Alison was born. There are several things I will always remember about Alison when she was young: 1. She used to call me the kissy uncle, refusing to give me a kiss and pushing me a way. She was only four and this would make me laugh and want to kiss her all the more, and 2. About the same age, she would walk with me hand in hand on the sidewalk near her house. After it had rained, if we came upon a puddle, she would bend over and dip her entire head in it, stand straight up, throw her hair back, and continue to walk. Have you ever seen something so funny that no sound comes out when you laugh? This was it. And it wasn't a one-time thing. She did it with every puddle she saw. Once we began to serve entrees at The Soup Kitchen, Ltd., this recipe was added to the menu. It was popular from the outset and remains so to this day.

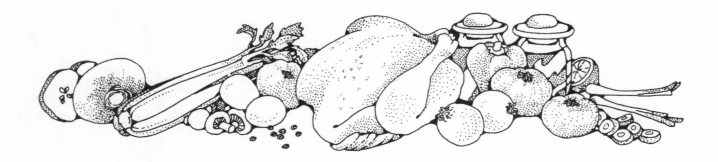

Serves 4

4 chicken breasts
8 cups of bread, cubed
1 cup of onions, chopped
1 cup of celery, chopped
4 oz of butter, 1 stick
1 cup of provolone cheese, cubed
1/2 lb of sweet Italian sausage,
    parboiled and cut into 1/4 inch
    rounds
1/2 cup of walnuts, chopped
1 1/2 cups of milk (as needed)
2 whole eggs, lightly beaten
1/4 cup of oil
3 tsp of garlic powder or fresh,
    chopped
1 Tbsp of poultry seasoning, or to
    taste
1 tsp of thyme
1 tsp of tarragon
1 tsp of salt
1 tsp of pepper

1. Wash chicken in salt water.
2. On medium heat, sauté onions and celery in butter.
3. Then, add poultry seasoning, thyme, and 2 tsp of
    garlic. Sauté for 5 minutes. Set aside.
4. In a large bowl, place bread, cheese, walnuts and
    sausage.
5. Combine cooked vegetables with bread mixture.
6. Next, add milk and mix well with hands.
7. Then, add lightly beaten eggs and mix well.
8. Salt and pepper to taste. Adjust all seasonings.
9. Place dressing in a well-greased baking dish.
10. Next, place chicken on top of the dressing.
11. Mix together oil, 1 tsp of garlic powder, salt, pepper
    and tarragon.
12. Brush top of chicken with oil concoction.
13. Bake at 350 for 90 minutes or until chicken's
    internal temperature reaches 180.

Wayne's hint ☞ I prefer the chicken with skin-on and bone-in. It makes for a more flavorful dish.

Chicken Gumbo

Serves 4–6

I like to add chopped pecans while cooking my rice in this recipe.

4 boneless, skinless chicken breasts cut into bite-size pieces2 cups of tomatoes, cubed (canned tomatoes are fine)
1 cup of green pepper, cubed
1 cup of red pepper, cubed
1 cup of onion, chopped
2 cups of corn, fresh or frozen, yellow or white
2 cups of okra, fresh or frozen, sliced thick
4 cups of chicken stock or 4 cups of water with 4 tsp of chicken bouillon granules
2 Tbsp of file gumbo
2 Tbsp of garlic powder or fresh, chopped
Olive oil as needed
Cayenne pepper to taste
Salt and Pepper to taste

1. Lightly sauté garlic, onion, red and green peppers in olive oil.
2. Add chicken stock and bring to a simmer.
3. Add raw chicken and cook for 10 minutes.
4. Add tomatoes and corn. Simmer for 5 minutes.
5. Add file gumbo.
6. Adjust seasoning cayenne pepper, salt and pepper.
7. Now, add okra last so not to become too gummy.
8. Simmer for 5 minutes and serve over rice.

Wayne's hint ☞ I make this dish in the winter all the time. Fresh tomatoes and okra are not always available. So, I reach for the canned tomatoes and frozen okra and it works just fine.

Wayne's Orzo

Orzo is pasta you will see used in many Greek dishes. It always amazes me that they can make pasta so small. This recipe uses cinnamon, which is a very Greek use of this spice. I used to think of cinnamon only for baking. But after incorporating it in side dishes and some main dishes, I have learned how versatile this spice can be. You will see it used often in this cookbook.

Serves 4–6

1–28 oz can of crushed tomatoes
1 cup of onion, chopped
1 Tbsp of garlic powder or fresh, chopped
1 lb of orzo pasta
1/2 Tbsp of sugar
1 tsp of cinnamon
Salt and Pepper to taste

1. Sauté onions until translucent.
2. Add crushed tomatoes, sugar and spices. Simmer for 5 to 10 minutes
3. Cook and drain orzo for about 11 minutes.
4. Add orzo to tomatoes and heat thoroughly.

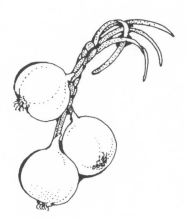

Wayne's hint ☞ I like grilled lamb, chicken, or shrimp to top this dish.

Chicken Pot Pie with Cheddar Cheese Biscuits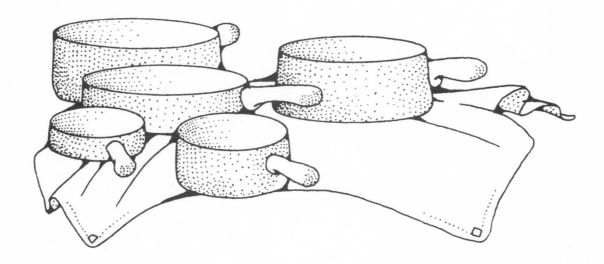

Even though we have made this at the restaurant for more than twenty years, reducing it in size has taken a year and a half of frustrating experimentation. Yvette, my assistant, thinks this is funny. Well, it's not funny. I've worked hard to make this complicated dish as simple as possible for you. It's been a comforting dish in my family for a long time, but for some reason I forgot to get this one written down for fewer portions. Since neither my mother nor grandmother is here anymore, I've struggled with the flavor, consistency, and topping. Today I've finally nailed it and I'm celebrating. Yeahhh! This works. I'm so happy to have it written down for the generations to come. I hope you enjoy this simplified version of chicken pot pie as much as I do. One of my biggest problems was the chicken. I didn't want to poach it before adding it to the pie, and I remained undecided about it for a very long time. Ms. Brenda always poached it at the restaurant. You'll see what I ended up doing. Ms. Brenda was right again.

Serves 4–5

1 1/2 lbs of boneless chicken
    breast
1 cup of peas, fresh or frozen
1 cup of lima beans or 1 cup of
    cut green beans
1 cup of corn, fresh or frozen
1 cup of onion, chopped fine
1 cup of carrot, chopped
1 cup of celery, sliced 1/4 of an
    inch thick
1 cup of half-and-half
1 cup of chicken stock or 1 cup of
    water with 1 tsp of chicken
    bouillon granules
2 oz of butter, 1/2 stick
1/4 oz of flour
2 tsp of thyme
1/4 tsp of garlic powder or fresh,
    chopped
1/4 tsp of ground red pepper

1. Cut chicken breast into bite-size pieces and poach
    for 6–8 minutes, remove from water and drain.
2. Sauté onions, carrots, celery, garlic, ground red
    pepper and thyme in butter until almost tender
    (5–10 minutes).
3. Add flour and cook for 3 more minutes.
4. Add chicken stock. Cook until it thickens.
5. Now add remaining vegetables. Allow to cook for
    5–8 minutes, until vegetables begin to soften
    (the mixture will be thick).
6. Add half-and-half. Cook until mixture is thoroughly
    heated.
7. Then, add chicken and cook for 3 minutes.
8. Place in 9x13 baking dish.
9. You can now cover with pastry crust or as I like to
    do top with cheddar cheese biscuits (see recipe
    on next page).
10. Bake at 375 for 25–35 minutes or until golden
    brown.

Wayne's hint ☞ Turn the page for the cheddar cheese biscuits. When you have enough
time, they're a great addition to the pot pie.

Cheddar Cheese Biscuits

2 cups of flour
2 tsp of baking powder
1/2 tsp of baking soda
1/2 tsp of salt
4 Tbsp of cold butter, cut into pieces
3 Tbsp of cold vegetable shortening (Crisco)
3/4 cup of buttermilk
1 cup of cheddar cheese

1. Place all dry ingredients in a large mixing bowl.
2. With a large whisk blend dry ingredients.
3. Cut butter and vegetable shortening into dry ingredients (I do it with my fingers until butter is well corporated into flour.).
4. Add cheese.
5. Add buttermilk and stir with fork until dough forms into moist clumps.
6. Transfer dough into a floured work surface.
7. Form into a ball and with a rolling pin roll 1/2 inch thick.
8. Cut into 15 rounds.
9. Place on top of pot pie and bake at 375 for 25–35 minutes.

Wayne's hint ☞ My assistant, Yvette, came up with a great idea to save time. If you don't have the time to do the biscuits, make the pot pie and just buy the biscuits. I believe that comfort food should be easy and if you have a lot of time, make the biscuits. If you don't, don't.

Codfish Cakes "Coddies"

At one time, Codfish cakes were sold at most bars and corner grocery stores in Baltimore City. You could buy them for a quarter. Coddies were also part of a Lenten tradition in most households. Now they are hard to find, but not hard to make. I love them with yellow mustard on Saltine crackers, served with Aunt Anna's peas and slaw.

Serves 4–6

2 cups of codfish, dried and boned
2 1/2 cups of mashed potatoes
2 whole eggs, beaten with cream
2 Tbsp of cream, beaten with eggs
1 Tbsp of parsley, chopped fine
3 Tbsp of onion, minced
Old Bay ® seasoning, a dash

1. **Soak the fish several hours or overnight, changing water several times. Drain off water.**
2. **Cover with fresh water and simmer until fish is tender.**
3. **Drain and finely flake with fork, let cool.**
4. **In large mixing bowl, combine codfish, mashed potatoes, onion and eggs.**
5. **Add parsley and Old Bay. Mix thoroughly.**
6. **Shape into cakes and fry in hot oil until golden brown.**

Wayne's hint ☞ It's very important to soak your fish. I forgot to tell my TV audience one day, and an elderly lady called me very angry because her cakes were too salty. She wanted her money refunded for the purchase of the cod, so I did. I'm spreading the word. Soak your fish!

Wayne's Corned Beef and Cabbage

There was a time when every corner bar or beer joint in Baltimore served up this dish on March 17. Patrons in the neighborhood gathered to drink green beer and eat this traditional St. Patrick's Day dish. Bess' Bar, which inspired this recipe, would add extra tables and line them up in rows, communal style. Irish music would be played. Heaping platters of corned beef, potatoes, and cabbage would be placed in front of the seated guests. There was no charge for the food, only the beer and liquor. Customers would waddle or stumble into the streets, happy to have partaken of the Irish Saint's Day. By that time, they had forgotten what they were celebrating. They just knew it was a holiday.

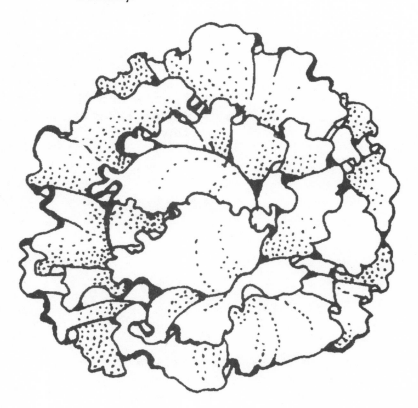

Serves 4

3 lbs of corned beef brisket
2 whole cloves
2 bay leaves
2 cups of potatoes, pared and cut
   in half
1 large head of cabbage, cut into 4
   wedges
2 tsp of garlic powder or fresh,
   chopped
1/2 cup of vinegar
1/2 cup of brown sugar, packed
1/2 cup of parsley for garnish
Salt and pepper to taste

1. **Place corned beef brisket in large pot. Cover with water.**
2. **Add garlic, cloves and bay leaves.**
3. **Bring to boil, reduce heat and simmer for 5 minutes.**
4. **Skim surface. Cover pot. Simmer 3 to 4 hours, or until corned beef is fork-tender.**
6. **Add potatoes during the last 25 minutes.**
7. **Add cabbage wedges during the last 15 minutes.**
8. **Cook vegetables until tender.**
9. **Remove brisket and slice across the grain.**
10. **Arrange slices on platter with cabbage and potatoes.**
11. **Sprinkle dish with parsley.**
12. **Don't forget to have a Guinness.**

Wayne's hint ☞ Wipe the corned beef with a damp paper towel to remove any excess brine. Leave the core in cabbage. It helps to keep it together.

Chicken Penne

Serves 4

4–6 oz boneless chicken breast, cubed
2 cups of half-and-half
8 oz of penne noodles
1/2 cup of cashews
2 Tbsp of olive oil
2 Tbsp of pesto sauce

1. Cook penne noodles according to instructions on package. Set aside.
2. Sauté chicken and cashews in olive oil.
3. Next, add half-and-half and simmer for 5 minutes.
4. Add pesto sauce and mix well.
5. Add penne noodles and cook for 3 minutes until cream is reduced.

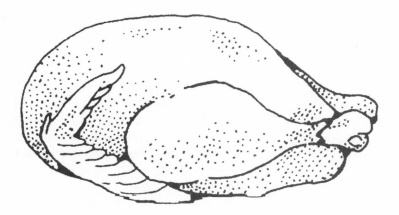

Wayne's hint ☞ Pesto sauce is not hard to make. It's a combination of oil, garlic, basil, and pine nuts. If you can't buy pesto, fresh basil and fresh garlic can be used.

Curry Chicken

Some people are not familiar with the use of curry in cooking. Curry is actually a combination of spices. In fact, I usually make my own. There are several types of curry powder. Madras curry is one of the hottest, and the typical kind you see in stores is less hot. I use curry the same way I use pepper or chili powder. It's the secret ingredient in my chili. It adds heat and flavor but is not overpowering if used in small amounts.

Serves 6

6 chicken breast fillets
1 cup of chicken stock or 1 cup of water with 1 tsp of chicken bouillon granules
1 cup of onion, chopped
4 medium white potatoes (Yukon gold), wedged
1 cup of tomatoes, crushed
1/2 cup of peas, frozen
2 Tbsp of olive oil
2 tsp of garlic powder or fresh, chopped
2 Tbsp of curry powder
1 Tbsp of ginger powder or fresh, chopped

1. **Cook potatoes separately until tender.**
2. **Sauté chicken breast in olive oil until brown.**
3. **Remove chicken and set aside.**
4. **In same pan, sauté onions and garlic.**
5. **Add peas, ginger, and curry.**
6. **Add tomatoes, stock and chicken breast.**
7. **Simmer for 15–20 minutes.**
8. **Drain potatoes and add to curry mixture.**

Wayne's hint ☞ This is a simple and easy dish especially for someone who is just beginning to experiment with the use of curry.

Delmonico Steak with Garlic Herb Glaze

This is a great topping that can be used on grilled fish, pork, or chicken. I like this better than a marinade, although marinades can be very useful especially with meats that need to be tenderized. Generally, I don't use marinades when cooking. This herb glaze adds a nice variety of flavors but will not take away from the Delmonico steak taste.

Serves 4

4 medium-sized New York Strip steaks
Glaze
3/4 cup of olive oil
1–2 cloves of garlic, chopped fine
2 heaping Tbsp of chopped herbs: rosemary, sage, dill, mint or basil
1/4 cup of balsamic vinegar
Salt and Pepper to taste

1. **Whisk together oil and balsamic vinegar.**
2. **Add garlic, salt and pepper.**
3. **Finally blend in the herbs and let stand for 15 minutes.**
4. **Grill meat to your desired wellness and place on platter.**
5. **Spoon glaze on top of meat.**

Wayne's hint ☞ Please use at least 3 of the 5 herbs, best to use all. Capers or pink peppercorns may be added as an option. I like capers. You can serve this steak with mashed potatoes and a side of sliced tomatoes and onions.

Wayne's Greek Shrimp

This was one of the first entrees to be added to the menu at The Soup Kitchen Ltd. It has stood the test of time. It is not trendy and for over twenty-five years I've served it in my home to many people who later requested the recipe. This is a meal in itself. Just add a bottle of wine and lots of bread to sop up the wonderful juices.

Serves 2–4

12–U15 shrimp, peeled and de-veined
6 oz of fresh spinach (baby or large leaf, torn not cut)
6 large tomatoes cut into 6 wedges each
4 oz of feta cheese
1/2 cup of extra virgin olive oil
1 tsp of garlic powder or fresh, chopped
1 tsp of dried oregano
1 tsp of fresh oregano, chopped (optional)
Salt and pepper to taste

1. Place spinach into a 10–inch pie pan (glass or ceramic) or a shallow casserole dish, mounding it slightly in the center.
2. Around the edge the dish, alternate shrimp and tomato wedges.
3. Arrange any extra shrimp or tomato in the center of the mound.
4. Crumble the feta cheese and sprinkle over entire dish.
5. In a small bowl, whisk together the dressing ingredients.
6. Drizzle the dressing over entire casserole using more or less to fit your taste.
7. Place in a pre-heated 350 oven for 20–30 minutes or until shrimp are pink.

Wayne's hint ☞ When adding your salt to this dish, remember, feta is very salty. Also, I think of Donna Hamilton when I think of this dish. It's one of her favorites.

Italian Sweet Sausage and Peppers

Italian sweet sausage is very versatile. You find it at street fairs served on a roll with peppers and onions, and in restaurants added to soups, pizza, and, as I suggest, served with polenta. As a main meal, I use 1/2" rounds. It makes it easier to eat. When I'm invited to Carolyn and Dino's for pasta, not only will there be her famous meatballs, but also the large saucepot containing massive amounts of Italian sweet sausage. I like this combination, and use it often when making tomato sauce.

Serves 4

2 lbs of Italian sweet sausage
2 cups of green peppers, julienne cut
2 cups of red peppers, julienne cut
1 cup of yellow onion, julienne cut
1 Tbsp of olive oil
Salt and pepper to taste

1. **Par boil sausage for 15 minutes. Cool and cut into 1/2–inch rounds or leave whole.**
2. **In oil, sauté onion, red and green peppers for about 5 minutes.**
3. **Salt and pepper.**
4. **Add sausage rounds and lightly brown.**
5. **Serve on a roll or as the main dish.**

Wayne's hint ☞ The reason you parboil your sausage is to remove most of the fat. If not, your dish will be way too greasy.

Ginger Pepper Steak

Serves 4–6

3 lbs of rib eye steak, cubed
2 cups of green peppers, cubed
1 cup of onion, chopped
2 cups of tomatoes, chopped
1/3 cup of cold water
3 Tbsp of soy sauce
1 tsp of red pepper flakes
3 Tbsp of dry sherry or brandy
1 Tbsp of ginger, fresh minced or powder
1 Tbsp of garlic powder or fresh, chopped
1 Tbsp of cornstarch
2 Tbsp of olive oil or as needed

1. In oil sauté steak cubes until brown on all sides using a large skillet.
2. Add green pepper, onion and red pepper flakes.
3. Next, add soy sauce, sherry, ginger and garlic (you may substitute liquor with stock).
4. Put a lid on pan, reduce heat and cook for 10–15 minutes.
5. In a separate bowl, mix cornstarch and cold water and whisk until smooth.
6. Add mixture to skillet stirring constantly, bring to a low boil until it thickens.
7. Add tomatoes and simmer for about 15 minutes with cover on.
8. Serve over rice or potatoes.

Wayne's hint ☞ Sauté beef a little at a time to ensure meat will brown and not steam. To accomplish this, you can remove after browning or, if your skillet is large enough, move browned meat to one side.

Grilled Chicken with Fennel and Asparagus

I love to make, serve, and eat this dish. It goes best over polenta.

Serves 6

6 boneless and skinless chicken breasts
2 fennel bulbs, trimmed, quartered, and cut into very thin slices
4 garlic cloves, peeled and sliced thin
1 lb of asparagus, sliced on a diagonal 1 inch cut
1–2 Tbsp of olive oil as needed
Salt and pepper to taste

1. **Place fennel and asparagus in a roasting pan or baking dish and top with garlic slivers.**
2. **Next, sprinkle olive oil over fennel, asparagus and garlic. Salt and pepper.**
3. **Roast in a 475 oven for 20–30 minutes or until fennel becomes tender.**
4. **Grill chicken and cut into strips.**
5. **Combine chicken, fennel, asparagus, garlic, and oil, toss.**
6. **Adjust seasoning, salt and pepper, and serve.**

Wayne's hint ☞ When making your polenta, use the recipe on the box and add 1/4 cup of Parmesan cheese and 1/4 cup of butter. I also like to use milk instead of water.

Pork Chops with Mustard Sauce and Potato Fingers ▰▰▰▰▰

This means Sundays in the Brokke family. The aroma spreading through the house takes me straight back to my youth. I serve this with sautéed spinach and a mustard sauce. Sometimes pork can be dry, so I added sauce to it—one of my mother's standard Sunday meals.

Serves 8

6 pork chops, boneless
2 large potatoes cut into 8 wedges each
1/4 cup of Parmesan cheese, grated
1 tsp of garlic powder or fresh, chopped
8 1/2 tsp of thyme
1/4 cup of olive oil
Salt and pepper to taste
Mustard Sauce
1/2 cup of cream or half-and-half
2 Tbsp of Dijon mustard
1 Tbsp of capers

1. Place chops in a shallow baking dish.
2. Arrange potatoes around meat.
3. Season with salt and pepper.
4. In separate bowl combine oil, garlic and thyme.
5. Brush oil mixture over meat and potatoes.
6. Next, sprinkle with cheese.
7. Bake at 375 until golden brown, approximately 1 1/2 hours.
8. Remove from baking dish and arrange on platter.
9. Combine the ingredients for mustard sauce with pan drippings, being sure to mix well.
10. Spoon sauce over potatoes and pork chops.

Wayne's hint ☞ I don't chew my bones. My father did. He'd add a little salt and chew away. I've always liked a boneless pork chop. If you like a bone, use a bone. I think we should put it on a T-Shirt.

Wayne's Guinness Beef Stew ▪▪▪▪▪▪▪▪▪▪▪▪▪▪

This stew can be made in advance and reheated. It is a great meal for St. Patrick's Day because of the Guinness. However, I like it as a cold winter day, Sunday meal.

Serves 4–6

2 lbs of beef, cubed
2 Tbsp of olive oil
2 cups of onions, chopped
2 cloves of garlic, crushed
1/4 cup of plain flour
1 cup beef stock or 1 cup of water with 1 tsp of beef bouillon granules
1 cup of Guinness
2 cups of carrots, sliced
1 tsp of thyme, dried or fresh
2 bay leaves
2 Tbsp of parsley, chopped
Salt and pepper to taste

1. **Sauté onions in olive oil, adding garlic once onions are golden brown. Cook for 1 minute.**
2. **Remove onions and garlic from the frying pan and set aside.**
3. **Brown meat in the same frying pan used for the onions**
4. **Reduce heat and add flour making sure the meat is coated.**
5. **Stir in beef stock to form a thick, creamy sauce.**
6. **Add Guinness and simmer**
7. **Add onions, garlic, bay leaves, carrots and thyme and season with salt and pepper.**
8. **Simmer and stir for 1–2 hours (without covering)**
9. **Use parsley to garnish.**

Wayne's hint ☞ Originally, this recipe called for dried prunes. So many people complained, I took them out. For myself, I like to add 1 cup to this recipe. Mmm, Mmm, good.

Lamb Chops with Blue Cheese Butter ▪▰▪▰▪▰▪▰▪▰▪▰

My father was stationed in Australia during WW II. He was a driver for a general; this meant he ate the same meals as his commanding officer. The meat most often served was lamb. My father said he had had enough of lamb in the service, and he forbade my mother to prepare lamb dishes. Since we never had lamb at home, it wasn't until I moved out on my own that I began to cook lamb. This was one of my first recipes. I like butter peas and a baked potato with my chops.

Serves 4

8 Lamb chops
Blue Cheese Butter
8 oz of Blue cheese or cheese Gorgonzola
** 4 oz of butter, 1 stick**
1/4 cup of pecans finely chopped
Pepper to taste

1. **Place cheese, pecans and butter in a bowl. Mash together with a fork.**
2. **When you get a good consistency add pepper to taste.**
3. **Grill or broil you chops to your taste.**
4. **Place a teaspoon of the blue cheese butter on top and allow to melt.**

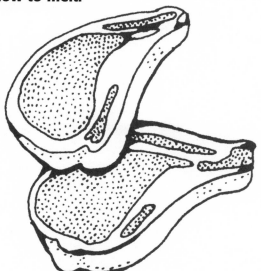

Wayne's hint ☞ Rib chops are my favorite, however, you can use loin chops.

Pot Roast

Pot roast is so simple it is often overlooked. My grandmother used chuck roast, and I enjoy that same cut of meat. She served this mostly Sundays when it wasn't a holiday—along with a variety of fresh vegetables. She lived to be ninety-five. I pray I have the same longevity.

Serves 4

5 lbs of chuck roast
1 cup of water
1 cup of onion, quartered
1 cup of carrots, cut into 1–inch rounds
1 cup of celery, cut 1 inch
2 cups of mushrooms, quartered
1 cup of tomatoes, chopped
1/2 cup of red wine, dry
1 tsp of rosemary
2 tsp of garlic powder or fresh, chopped
2 Tbsp of olive oil
Salt and pepper to taste

1. Season beef with salt and pepper.
2. It is very important to have your pan very hot so that you can sear the beef. Approximately 3 to 5 minutes on each side.
3. In a roasting pan, sear beef in oil until brown on both sides.
4. Add vegetables, garlic and rosemary.
5. Add wine and water.
6. Cover and bake at 300 for 2 1/2 hours or until meat is fork tender.

Wayne's hint ☞ There are a lot wonderful salad recipes in this cookbook that will complement this dish nicely. I especially suggest the watercress or the broccoli.

Quick and Easy Macaroni and Cheese Three Ways ▪▪▪▪▪

Ms. Brenda gave me this recipe. It seemed far too easy, so I tried a taste test with the staff at WBAL TV in Baltimore. I presented Ms. Brenda's simple recipe along with my more difficult one. Hers won hands down. Everyone said it tasted cheesier. Needless to say, I beg to differ.

Serves 6

1–16 oz box of uncooked elbow macaroni
2 cups of tomatoes, chopped (optional)
2 cups of broccoli, chopped (optional)
1 lb of Italian sweet sausage, parboiled and cut into 1/2 inch slices (optional)
4 oz of butter, 1 stick
1 cup of milk
16 oz of shredded cheese
Salt and pepper to taste

1. Cook and drain macaroni according to the directions on the box.
2. Place cooked macaroni in mixing bowl.
3. On medium heat, stir together milk and butter until butter is melted.
4. Stir in the shredded cheese and allow it to melt.
5. Add cheese to macaroni and toss.
6. If you are going to add broccoli, tomatoes, or sausage this is the time to do it.
7. Transfer the mixture to a greased baking dish.
8. Sprinkle with breadcrumbs or Parmesan cheese and bake at 350 for 10 minutes. To be honest with you, I place it in the dish and serve it. It's hot and creamy enough to go right to the table.
9. Adjust seasoning with salt and pepper.

Wayne's hint 🖝 It *is* easy, so I've taken the time to add tomatoes, or sausage, or broccoli. They all work great. I prefer tomatoes.

Meatballs

Meatballs remind me of going to school at Our Lady of Pompeii in Highlandtown. The school was surrounded by row houses with the classic Baltimore white marble steps that housed families of Italian descent. My family couldn't afford restaurants when I was a child. But in that neighborhood there was a restaurant that served meatball subs. Also, there was a penny store, as it was called, that sold penny candy, pickled onions, pretzels, and religious items. I always saved my money from doing chores for three things: 1. Being a good Catholic, I wanted a statue of Saint Theresa of the little flower; 2. Liking the combination, I would get a pickled onion with a large pretzel; and 3. Coveting it the most of all, I would get a meatball sub. To acquire the sub from the establishment that only seated its patrons, I had to go in and ask if I could get it to take out. At that time, not many places did carryout. They would always make an exception for me. I made sure I didn't impose on them very often, which made that meatball sub a very special treat. They would take a whole loaf of Italian bread, cut off one end, dig out the center, and insert six to eight large, luscious meatballs that had been simmering in a sweet, rich tomato sauce.

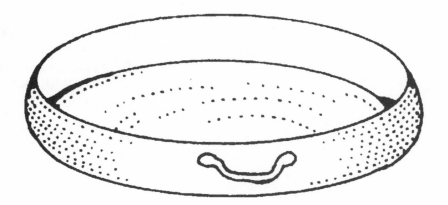

Serves 4–6 as appetizer

1 lb of ground beef
1 lb of ground pork
2 eggs, beaten
1/2 cup of onion, finely chopped
1/2 cup of crushed crackers
1/4 cup of ketchup
1 Tbsp of Worcestershire sauce
1/4 tsp of crushed red pepper
1 tsp of garlic
1/4 tsp each of salt and pepper

1. In large mixing bowl, combine all the ingredients thoroughly.
2. Then shape into meatballs.
3. Place on a lightly greased cookie sheet.
4. Bake for 35 minutes at 375 until brown.
5. Add to a sauce or cool and freeze for later use.

Wayne's hint ☞ These meatballs, when cooled, can be put into a zippered freezer bag until needed. They can be used for sandwiches, sauces, or as an appetizer.

Maryland Crab Cakes

Here in Maryland, we are very proud of our crab cakes. They may differ only slightly in ingredients, but Old Bay® is in every recipe. Whether fried or broiled, ours are the best. The worst crab cake made in Maryland, to me, is always better than any made in another state. My grandmother gave me this recipe. She used claw meat instead of back fin. She always enjoyed the dark meat of the crab. I like it both ways.

Serves 4–6

1 lb of crabmeat, back fin
1 egg
3 Tbsp of crackers, crushed
3 Tbsp of mayonnaise
1 Tbsp of mustard, yellow
1 Tbsp of parsley, chopped
1 tsp of Worcestershire sauce
1 tsp of Old Bay®

1. **Gently pick through crabmeat to remove shells, then set aside.**
2. **Beat egg then mix in mayonnaise.**
3. **Next, add parsley, mustard, Worcestershire, and Old Bay® to mixture.**
4. **Lightly toss together crackers and crab meat.**
5. **Gently, combine crab and mayonnaise mixture, making sure not to over work or mash crabmeat.**
6. **Form into round patties and place in shallow frying pan.**
7. **Brown on both sides over low heat or as I like to do, place on cookie sheet and broil until brown.**

Wayne's hint ☞ Recently, just this past Christmas, in fact, I couldn't find fresh crabmeat. At Arundel Seafood on Mountain Road a young man suggested and guaranteed the flavor his pasteurized all lump crabmeat. It was $25 a pound! I would have to say it was worth every penny. The miracles of modern technology never cease to amaze me. The flavor was as good as fresh.

Orange Garlic Chicken

Serves 4

4 boneless, skinless chicken breast

Sauce
1 cup of mandarin oranges with juice
1/4 cup of dry sherry
1 Tbsp of brown sugar
1 Tbsp of fresh rosemary, chopped fine
1 tsp of garlic powder or fresh, chopped fine

1. **Drain mandarin oranges and set a side.**
2. **Combine orange juice, sherry, sugar, rosemary, and garlic (If you like garlic as I do you can add as much as you can handle.)**
3. **Whisk until smooth.**
4. **Next, add mandarin oranges.**
5. **Grill or pan-fry chicken breasts.**
6. **Brush the chicken with sauce a few minutes before removing from grill.**
7. **When serving, pour an ample amount of sauce over chicken.**

Wayne's hint ☞ I like serving this dish with a combination of wild and brown rice and broccoli with lemon and butter.

Wayne's Pork and Sauerkraut

Serves 4–6

2 lb bag of sauerkraut
1 cup of apple, chopped
1 Tbsp of brown sugar
1 tsp of caraway seed
1 tsp of celery seed
1/2 tsp of coriander
1 tsp of fennel seed
1 1/2 cups of chicken stock or 1 1/2 cups of water
    with 1 1/2 tsp of chicken bouillon granules
2–3 lb center cut pork roast
Garlic Herb Glaze
1/4 cup of olive oil
1/2 tsp of garlic powder or fresh, chopped
1/4 tsp of thyme
Salt and pepper to taste

1. Wash sauerkraut and place in large mixing bowl.
2. Add apple, brown sugar, caraway, celery, coriander, fennel seed and chicken stock. Mix well.
3. Place mix in baking dish
4. Next, place roast on top sauerkraut.
5. Whisk together olive oil, garlic, thyme, salt and pepper.
6. Brush pork with glaze.
7. Cover loosely with aluminum foil and place in oven at 350 untilpork is done (about 20 minutes per pound).
8. Remove foil for the last 30 minutes of baking so the pork will brown.

Wayne's hint ☞ I think its important to wash the sauerkraut to remove excess brine and bitterness. The apple is important to add sweetness against the tartness of the sauerkraut.

Roasted Chicken with Honey Mustard Sauce ▰▱▰▱▰▱▰▱▰

Serves 4–6

Serve with cornbread, get your
    fingers into the sauce and pick
    up the cornbread—heaven.

3–4 lbs of whole chicken roaster
1 stalk of celery cut in thirds
1 carrot cut in thirds
1 small onion cut in half
I clove of garlic
1 Tbsp of thyme
2 Tbsp of olive oil
Salt and pepper to taste
Honey mustard sauce
2 1/4 cups of Dijon mustard
3/4 cup of honey
1/4 cup of vegetable oil

1. Rinse chicken inside and out under cold running
    water.
2. Place celery, carrot, onion, garlic, thyme and salt
    and pepper inside.
3. Tie the legs together with string.
4. Rub outside with oil and salt and pepper.
5. Put chicken in roasting pan, and roast in a 350
    oven for 20 minutes per pound, occasionally
    basting with pan juices.
6. Mix the honey mustard sauce.
7. The last 15 minutes coat the chicken with the
    honey mustard sauce.
8. The chicken is done when you prick the leg with a
    knife and the juice runs clear.

Wayne's hint ☞ This is the recipe for the honey mustard sauce I use at my restaurant. You enjoy now, because I won't give you the recipe for my BBQ sauce. I like serving cornbread with this. Another plug: my cornbread can be purchased from our website, waynecooks.com.

Scalloped Oysters

Serves 4–6

2 pints of oysters in liquor
1 1/2 cups of milk
3 cups of crackers, coarsely crushed
1/2 tsp of Old Bay ® seasoning, if not available use
    1/4 tsp of nutmeg
4 oz of butter, 1 stick
Salt and pepper to taste

1. In a buttered 7x11 or 2 quart casserole dish, place crackers then oysters.
2. Alternate layers of crackers and oysters.
3. Dot each layer with butter pats, salt and pepper.
4. Finish with layer of cracker crumbs.
5. Whisk Old Bay ® into milk.
6. Add milk until liquid almost reaches top of casserole.
7. Dot with remaining butter.
8. Bake at 350 until brown (approximately 30–40 minutes).

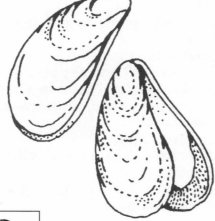

Wayne's hint ☞ I served this as part of the feast of The Seven Fishes last Christmas Eve. Instead of milk, I used half-and-half, which made for a richer dish.

Baltimore Creamed Crab with Asparagus and Biscuits ▰▰▰▰

Serves 6

1 lb of asparagus cut into 1/2–inch slices
1 lb of crabmeat, back fin
1/2 cup of shredded cheddar cheese
1/3 cup of flour
1/3 cup of butter
2 tsp of dry mustard
1/4 tsp of nutmeg
2 tsp of onion powder
2 drops of Tabasco sauce
4 cups of half-and-half
Salt and pepper to taste

1. Melt butter, add the flour and stir until smooth. (8 minutes)
2. Add cold half-and-half to flour and butter mixture whisking occasionally.
3. Bring to a simmer and add nutmeg, dry mustard and onion powder.
4. Add crab, cheese and asparagus.
5. Adjust seasoning with salt, pepper and Tabasco sauce. Heat thoroughly.
6. Serve over toast or biscuits.

Wayne's hint ☞ My mother always served the creamed asparagus over toast as a breakfast dish. I converted it to a dinner entree by adding crabmeat and putting it over biscuits.

Shrimp Amanda

This dish was created for my niece Amanda Rose, who was named after my mother, Rose. It comes from the early days when entrees were added to our menu. My mother always wanted a child with dark hair, blue eyes, and olive skin: in reality, someone who resembled her. My mother had four children who were towheads: blonde with fair skin. When I first saw Amanda she was only five minutes old, a beautiful dark-haired, blue-eyed girl, who looked at me and stuck out her tongue. From that first joyful moment we have had an unyielding bond. To this day she loves to hear me tell this story, which, of course, I love to do.

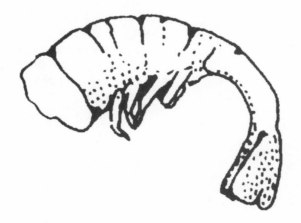

Serves 4–6

2 lbs of shrimp, peeled with tails
on
1/2 cup of chicken stock or 1/2
cup of water with 1/2 tsp of
chicken bouillon granules
1/2 lb of penne pasta
8 oz of feta cheese, cubed
1–28 oz can of whole tomatoes,
hand crushed
1 cup of red pepper, julienne cut
1 cup of green pepper, julienne
cut
1 cup of onion, julienne cut
1 Tbsp of sugar
1 Tbsp of garlic powder or fresh,
chopped
1 Tbsp of basil, dried
1 Tbsp of parsley, chopped
1 tsp of crushed red pepper
1 Tbsp of olive oil or as needed

1. In olive oil, sauté onions, peppers, and garlic until tender.
2. Add chicken stock and tomatoes.
3. Add sugar, basil, parsley and crushed red pepper.
4. Simmer for 15–20 minutes.
5. Add shrimp and simmer for 15 minutes.
6. Cook pasta, and then add to sauce. Simmer for about 3 minutes.
7. Place in a serving dish.
8. Then, sprinkle with feta cheese and serve.

Wayne's hint ☞ I like to use large shrimp in this recipe. I serve it with a mixed green salad with thinly sliced onion and an oil and vinegar dressing.

Wayne's Meatloaf

Meatloaf is one of those dishes that should be simple and easy. It should provide enough flavor and aroma to remind us of our mother's cooking (even if she burned it—I still liked the burned ends). We have served this recipe at The Soup Kitchen Ltd. for more than twenty years. Whether it's lunch or dinner, rain or snow, sun or clouds, happy or sad, this is food that comforts us and gives us the feeling that Mom is in the kitchen and we are taken care of.

Serves 4–6

3 lbs of ground beef
1 egg
1/2 cup of ketchup for meatloaf
1/2 cup of ketchup for ribbon (to top meatloaf)
1 cup of onion, chopped fine
1 cup of green pepper, chopped fine
1 cup of crackers, crushed
2 tsp of garlic powder or fresh, chopped
1 Tbsp of Worcestershire sauce
Salt and pepper to taste

1. **Combine all ingredients with hands until well blended.**
2. **Shape into loaf and place in baking dish.**
3. **Top with a ribbon of ketchup.**
4. **Bake at 375 for 40 minutes.**

Wayne's hint ☞ To make mini meatloafs, try using a muffin pan, large or small. I think it's nice when a person gets their own mini meatloaf.

Shrimp Creole

Serves 4–6

2 lbs of shrimp
2 cups of chicken stock or 2 cups of water with 2
   tsp of chicken bouillon granules
1–28 oz can of whole tomatoes, hand crushed
1–28 oz can of crushed tomatoes
2 cups of celery, chopped medium
2 cups of onions, chopped medium
2 cups of green Pepper, cubed
2 tsp of garlic powder or fresh, chopped
4 oz of margarine
4 oz of flour
1 Tbsp of sugar
4 oz of Worcestershire Sauce
2 Tbsp of Tabasco
2 Tbsp of Cajun spice
1/2 Tbsp of white pepper
1 bay leaf
1 Tbsp of salt

1. In large deep skillet, melt margarine.
2. Add onions and celery. Sauté until translucent.
3. Next, add flour and cook for 5 minutes.
4. Add tomatoes.
5. Stir in chicken stock, sugar, Worcestershire sauce,
   tabasco, cajun spice, white pepper, bay leaf and
   salt.
6. Add shrimp and green pepper and allow to simmer
   for 5 minutes.
7. Adjust seasoning with salt and pepper and serve.
8. Serve over rice.

Wayne's hint ☞ You may also use clams, scallops, oysters, and mussels.

Stuffed Red and Yellow Peppers

Serves 4

2 lbs of ground beef or turkey
2 yellow peppers, tops removed
2 red peppers, tops removed
1 cup of onion, chopped fine
1 cup of celery, chopped fine
1 cup of rice, cooked
1 small jalapeno pepper, chopped fine
1 tsp of cilantro
2 tsp of garlic powder or fresh, chopped
1 tsp of Tabasco

1. **In a large bowl, combine ground beef with onion, jalapeno, cilantro, garlic, Tabasco, celery, and rice.**
2. **Remove tops of peppers and fill with mixture.**
3. **Put tops back on.**
4. **Bake at 350 for 35–45 minutes.**

Wayne's hint ☞ I prefer using red or yellow peppers because they're sweet. They don't have the bitterness of green peppers when cooked.

Baked Rock Fish with Tomatoes and Onions

On Good Friday, my father would get a rockfish from one of his fisherman friends that my mother would prepare for the Holy Day meal. It was a real treat because fresh fish was a rarity in our home, and my mother's presentation of the dish was always so beautiful.

Serves 4–6

1–3 to 4 lb Maryland Rockfish, cleaned, head removed, skin-on, not filleted
1 clove of garlic, chopped
1 Tbsp of dill, fresh, frozen or dried
2 Tbsp of olive oil
1 cup of tomato, sliced
1 cup of onion, cut into 1/2–inch slices
Salt and white pepper to taste

1. Wash fish with cold water.
2. Open cavity and season with salt and pepper.
3. Cut tomato into 1/2–inch slices.
4. Cut onion into 1/2–inch slices.
5. Mix oil, dill and garlic.
6. In open cavity alternate tomatoes and onion slices.
7. Top tomato and onions with oil mixture.
8. Close cavity and coat the top of fish with a little olive oil, salt, and pepper.
9. Place in baking dish and bake at 350 for 20 to 25 minutes.

Wayne's hint ☞ Some people like to leave the head and tail on when cooking fish. This is to add flavor to the dish. I see the fish staring back at me, and I can't do it. So, I always remove the head and tail. I find the flavor just fine.

Yvette's Creamy Shrimp Scampi

As this book is being written, the recipes are being tested and double-checked in my kitchen. This thin sauce has lots of flavor and compliments the shrimp and spinach combination. Yvette, who is a whiz on the computer and is converting my hand-written notes into the manuscript, has a fondness for white sauce. Today, pasta is on the agenda, so I create and dedicate this recipe to her. You have to understand that Yvette doesn't eat much of what I cook, especially my pickled eggs. So, it is a pleasure to watch her savor this dish—a thank you for all her flexibility and her willingness to interpret my hieroglyphics. So, thank you Yvette, XOXOXO.

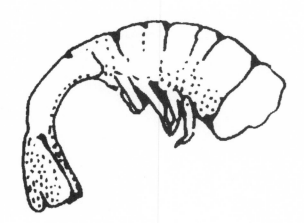

Serves 4

1 lb of spinach, frozen
8 oz of ziti pasta
2 lbs of shrimp (peeled and de-
    veined)
2 Tbsp of oil
2 Tbsp of butter, unsalted
1 cup of chicken stock or 1 cup of
    water with 1 tsp of chicken
    bouillon granules
1 cup of half-and-half
2 tsp of garlic powder or fresh,
    chopped
1/2 tsp of red pepper
1/2 cup of Parmesan cheese
1 tsp of salt

1. Cook pasta according to directions and drain. Set aside.
2. In a pan, melt butter with oil.
3. Next, add garlic and red pepper.
4. Add chicken stock. Bring to a simmer and add spinach.
5. Then, add shrimp. Continue cooking for about 5 minutes.
6. Add half-and-half.
7. Add pasta to the same pan. Simmer for about 3 minutes.
8. Place in a serving bowl and garnish with Parmesan cheese.

Wayne's hint ☞ I like using ziti because the sauce goes into the tube of the pasta. Also, using half-and-half will make a thinner sauce. To make a thicker sauce use heavy cream a.k.a. whipping cream. I like the whipping cream. It reduces nicely.

Vegetables

Asparagus with an Herb Dressing ▪▪▪▪▪▪▪▪▪▪▪▪▪▪▪

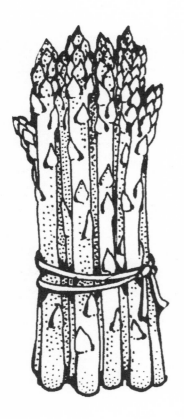

Serves 4

1 lb of asparagus
1 large sweet red pepper, julienne cut
  (approximately 2 cups)
Dressing
1/2 cup of olive oil
1/4 cup of balsamic vinegar
1/4 cup yellow onion, chopped fine
1 tsp of garlic powder or fresh, chopped
2 Tbsp of basil, fresh thinly sliced
1 Tbsp of fresh ginger, chopped
Salt and pepper to taste

1. In a pot, cover asparagus with water and cook until you reach desired tenderness.
2. Whisk olive oil and balsamic vinegar until well blended.
3. Add ginger, basil, garlic, onion, salt and pepper, and let stand for 15 minutes.
4. Drain asparagus and place in serving dish.
5. Top with red sweet pepper.
6. Pour dressing over asparagus and red pepper, then serve.

Wayne's hint ☞ If you don't have fresh basil and asparagus, don't make this recipe.

Baked Acorn Squash

Three miles from Gibson Island, just off the Chesapeake Bay, there is a horse farm that used to be a vegetable farm. Cindy, along with her husband, children, parents, and aunts and uncles, worked the farm and ran a produce stand. It was just a short trip to the Holt's Farm for great vegetables. The beauty of having them close-by was that I could focus on gardening flowers. When the Holts would finish work in early evening, there was a cash box to deposit your money and be on your way. Honor system. What a nice way to live. This recipe they handed out for all to enjoy. Thank you, Cindy and family for all the years I didn't have to plant tomatoes or acorn squash.

Serves 4

2 large acorn squash cut in half
2/3 cup of cracker crumbs
1/3 cup of pecans, chopped
1/3 cup of butter
3 Tbsp of brown sugar
1/4 tsp of cinnamon
1/4 tsp of nutmeg
1/4 tsp of vanilla
1/2 tsp of salt

1. **Cut squash in half remove seeds and fiber, set aside.**
2. **In a pot, melt butter and blend in all other ingredients.**
3. **Spoon into each half.**
4. **Place squash in baking dish.**
5. **Pour water to 1/4–inch depth.**
6. **Cover with aluminum foil.**
7. **Bake at 400 for 30–45 minutes or until tender.**

Wayne's hint ☞ This is a dish that children will enjoy making. I find if they help, they will definitely eat what they make.

Oyster Stuffing

My mother was quite famous for making this stuffing. Her biggest fan was my sister-in-law, Brenda's father. I would always enjoy Thanksgiving morning when he arrived to collect his casserole full of oyster stuffing made especially for him. I chuckle to think of his name—and my father's name. Imagine, my father's name was Olaf and his name was Orlaf. They called him Burton, which was his last name, and called my father Brock, short for Brokke. I guess they really didn't like Orlaf and Olaf. Whatever he was called, Orlaf or Burton, he always got his oyster stuffing, and my mother, Rose, would always get showered with his compliments. What a nice way to start a holiday.

Serves 6–8

8 cups of bread, cubed
1 cup of onion, chopped
1 cup of celery, chopped
4 oz of butter, 1 stick
1 pint of oysters, drained
1 1/2 cup of milk (as needed)
2 whole eggs, lightly beaten
1 tsp of garlic powder or fresh,
    chopped
1 Tbsp of poultry seasoning or to
    taste
1 tsp of thyme
1 tsp of salt
1 tsp of pepper

1. On medium heat, sauté onions and celery in butter.
2. Then, add poultry seasoning, thyme, and garlic. Sauté for 5 minutes. Set aside. Enjoy the aromas of the herbs and spices.
3. In a large bowl, combine bread with cooked vegetables.
4. Next, add milk and mix well with hands.
5. Then, add lightly beaten eggs and mix well.
6. Gently fold in oysters.
7. Adjust all seasonings with salt and pepper.
8. Place dressing in a well-greased baking dish.
9. Bake at 350 for 35–45 minutes or until golden brown.

Wayne's hint ☞ I drain my oysters. But, if you want a stronger oyster flavor, use the liquor.

Stewed Tomatoes

This dish reminds me of Grandmother and Mother. They would serve stewed tomatoes with fish on Fridays along with macaroni and cheese. They're hard to find in restaurants today, and rarely seen at family dinner tables as well. Try them, I think you'll like them.

Serves 4–6

1–28 oz can of whole tomatoes, hand crushed
1/2 cup of water
1 cup of white bread, small cubes
1 cup of yellow onion, minced
1 cup of celery
2 tsp of Worcestershire sauce
2 tsp of sugar
1/4 tsp of red pepper
1/2 tsp of garlic powder or fresh, chopped
2 oz of butter, 1/2 stick
Salt and pepper to taste

1. Sauté onions and celery in butter until almost soft.
2. Add garlic, red pepper, Worcestershire sauce and sugar.
3. Add tomatoes and water.
4. Cook for 10 to 15 minutes.
5. Add bread cubes. Allow to cook for another 15 minutes.
6. Salt and pepper to taste.
7. Place in serving dish. Dot with butter and serve.

Wayne's hint ☞ I like using one or two-day-old bread when making this recipe. In the summertime I use fresh Maryland tomatoes. You should definitely try yellow tomatoes. Oh, don't forget, to serve with fish and the macaroni and cheese.

Baked White Beans

Serves 4–6

2–15 oz cans of cannellini beans, white kidney
1 cup of onion, chopped fine
1/2 cup of celery, chopped fine
1/2 cup of Parmesan cheese
1 Tbsp of olive oil
1 Tbsp of rosemary, removed from stem
1 Tbsp of garlic powder or fresh, chopped
Salt and white pepper to taste
Italian sweet sausage (precooked) cut into 1/2
    rounds (optional)

1. Sauté onions, celery, and garlic in oil.
2. Add rosemary.
3. Add white beans and simmer for 5 minutes.
4. Adjust seasoning with salt and white pepper.
5. Place in a baking dish and top with Parmesan
    cheese.
6. Bake at 350 for 15 minutes.

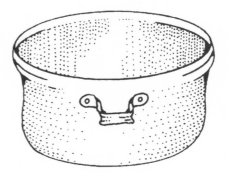

Wayne's hint ☞ White pepper is used so as not to have black specks. But remember, white pepper is a hotter pepper.

Wayne's Black-eyed Peas and Collard Greens ░░░░░░░

A Baltimore tradition in many households for New Year's was to have black-eyed peas, which are a symbol of good luck. Greens: collard, kale, or mustard symbolize prosperity. Fish for intelligence, usually fried catfish. This is a wonderful way to start a new year. For me, it's more palatable than what my family would serve: pickled herring and lutefisk, a Norwegian cod with an aroma that could be rated toxic.

Serves 4–6

Black-eyed Peas
1 ham hock or 1/2 lb of bacon, cut into 1/2 inch slices
2 tsp of garlic powder or fresh, chopped
1 lb of dried black-eyed peas
1 bay leaf
1 cup of onion, finely chopped
5–6 cups of water
1/2 cup of celery, finely chopped
Salt and pepper to taste

1. Rinse and sort beans in a colander under cold water. Black-eyed peas have thin skins so you will not need to soak.
2. In a large stockpot, place ham hock and cover with water to 1 inch above hock. Bring to boil.
3. Add onion, celery, garlic and bay leaf.
4. Reduce heat and simmer for 20 minutes, then add peas.
5. Cook on a medium heat until desired tenderness is reached, about 45 minutes.
6. Add salt and pepper to taste.

Greens: Collard, Mustard, or Kale
2 lbs of fresh mixed greens
2 quarts of water
1 ham hock
2 tsp of garlic powder or fresh, chopped
1 cup of onion, finely chopped
2 tsp of chicken bouillon
2 tsp of Tabasco
1 Tbsp of sugar
Salt and pepper to taste

1. **Rinse greens under cold water, removing hard stems or dried leaf.**
2. **In a large stockpot, place ham hocks and cover with water, bring to boil.**
3. **Skim froth from pot.**
4. **Add garlic, onion, bouillon, Tabasco, sugar, salt and pepper.**
5. **Reduce heat and simmer for 20 minutes. Add greens and cook on low heat for a long time could be up to 2 hours.**
6. **I have tried for years to duplicate Sherly Billy and Mona Tillery's Greens. I have found that cooking them to death came close. In fact, I think I like these better. Don't tell the girls.**
7. **Salt and pepper to taste.**

Wayne's hint ☞ You can buy black-eyed peas fresh and they won't need soaking. Also I add just enough water to cover the beans, making sure not to add too much water so that they don't become waterlogged. While cooking, I'm constantly adjusting the water level.

Brussels Sprouts with Walnut Butter ░░░░░░░░░░░░

I never used to like Brussels sprouts. One night several years ago, I awoke from a deep, peaceful sleep with a craving for Brussels sprouts. Go figure. I rushed to the store to buy one of those round containers with the cellophane protective top with the rubber band around it. I went home after work and cooked and ate the entire package to satisfy my craving. After that, I didn't like Brussels sprouts again until the craving came back. I think the Brussels sprouts gods were trying to possess me. Eventually, the cravings became more evenly dispersed. And now, I love Brussels sprouts all the time. I once prepared this recipe for a guest from Italy. Several weeks later she sent me an e-mail requesting the recipe. Now I'm international—ain't that something?

Serves 4

1 lb of Brussels sprouts
6 Tbsp of butter
1 cup of walnuts, chopped
2 Tbsp of brown sugar
2 tsp of Tabasco
Salt and pepper to taste

1. Wash Brussels sprouts and remove bottoms.
2. Cut in half or if small leave whole and score bottoms.
3. Place Brussels sprouts in pot and cover with water to 1 inch above sprouts.
4. Simmer for 15–20 minutes or to your desired tenderness.
5. In a separate pot, melt butter and brown sugar. Add Tabasco.
6. Add chopped walnuts to butter mix and cook for 5 minutes.
7. Drain sprouts and place in serving dish.
8. Adjust seasoning with salt and pepper.
9. Pour butter mixture over top, toss and serve.

Wayne's hint ☞ I think the smaller the Brussels sprouts the more tender the dish.

Sautéed Red Cabbage

This is a wonderful fall or winter side dish that I serve with either pork or beef roast along with parsley potatoes.

Serves 4–6

8 cups of red cabbage, cored and shredded
1/2 cup of water
2 oz of butter (1/2 stick)
1/2 cup of yellow onion, finely chopped
1/4 cup of red wine vinegar
1/4 cup of sugar
2 tsp of Tabasco
1 tsp of caraway seed
1 tsp of garlic powder or fresh, chopped
Salt and pepper to taste

1. Melt butter in pan and sauté onions.
2. Add shredded cabbage, garlic, Tabasco and caraway seed. Simmer for 10–15 minutes.
3. Dissolve sugar into vinegar. Add to cabbage.
4. Add water. Cover pan and simmer slowly for about 1 hour.
5. Next, add salt and pepper.
6. Place in a serving dish, add 2 pats of butter and serve.

Wayne's hint ☞ You need to watch the amount of liquid so that the cabbage will not dry out. Add more as needed during cooking.

Corn Creole with Okra

Serves 4–6

2 cups of corn, fresh or frozen
1 cup of okra, sliced, fresh or
   frozen
2 cups of whole tomatoes, hand
   crushed
1 cup of green pepper, chopped
1 cup of onion, chopped
2 oz of butter, 1/2 stick
1 Tbsp of flour
1 tsp of Cajun spice or to taste
1 Tbsp of Worcestershire sauce
1/2 tsp of garlic powder or fresh,
   chopped
1/2 tsp of cumin
1/4 tsp of ground red pepper
1 tsp of sugar

1. Sauté onion and green pepper in butter.
2. When onion is tender add flour and cook for 3
   minutes.
3. Next, add tomatoes, ground red pepper,
   Worcestershire sauce, sugar, cumin, garlic and
   Cajun spice.
4. Simmer for 5 minutes.
5. Add corn and continue to cook for 5–10 minutes.
6. Add okra.
7. Serve over rice or as a side dish.

Wayne's hint ☞ Add the okra just before serving so it doesn't become too slippery.

Wayne's Corn Pudding

Serves 4–6

2 cups of corn, fresh or frozen
1 Tbsp of flour
1 Tbsp of sugar
3 eggs
1/2 tsp of salt
1/4 tsp of cumin
1/4 tsp of ground red pepper
1/4 tsp of cilantro
2 oz of butter, 1/2 stick, at room temperature
1 cup of milk or half-and-half

1. Place all ingredients except corn into a blender, being sure butter is at room temperature. Mix well.
2. Place corn into the bottom of a buttered 8x8–baking dish.
3. Next, pour mixture on top.
4. Bake in a 350 over for 45 minutes or until golden brown.

Wayne's hint ☞ If your corn is fresh and sweet like it is in the summer, I would reduce or eliminate the sugar.

Wayne's Broiled Eggplant ▪▫▪▫▪▫▪▫▪▫▪▫▪▫▪▫▪▫▪▫▪▫▪▫

This is a great recipe to serve immediately or keep in the refrigerator for another day. I like adding it to antipasti or serving it as a side dish. I also cover it with tomato sauce and top with a little Parmesan cheese. But my favorite is on a ham sandwich; instead of tomato I use the broiled eggplant. These are some of my favorite ways to use eggplant. I'll leave it up to you to create your own.

Serves 2–4

1 medium eggplant, sliced into 1/2 inch rounds
1 cup of olive oil
1 Tbsp of fresh basil, chopped
1 Tbsp of fresh rosemary, chopped
2 tsp of garlic powder or fresh, chopped
Salt and pepper to taste

1. **Mix oil with basil, rosemary, garlic, salt and pepper and let mixture stand for 10 minutes. This gives seasoning and herbs time to blend with olive oil.**
2. **Brush both sides of eggplant with herb oil.**
3. **Place eggplant on cookie sheet.**
4. **Broil until eggplant turns golden brown, approximately 10 minutes.**

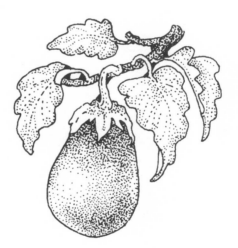

Wayne's hint ☞ This recipe can be used on an outside or inside grill; cook for about 3 minutes on each side.

The Perfect Mashed Potatoes ▪▪▪▪▪▪▪▪▪▪▪▪▪▪▪▪▪▪▪▪▪

Indeed, these are the perfect mashed potatoes. There are several variations on this recipe. Basil Mashed Potatoes, just add 1/3 cup of fresh, very thinly sliced basil. For Bacon and Cheddar Cheese Mashed Potatoes add 1/2 cup of crumbled bacon and 1 cup of cheddar cheese. Parmesan Mashed Potatoes add 1 cup of cheese. These are just a few, but use your imagination to create *your* perfect mashed potato recipe.

Serves 4–6

4 cups of potatoes, washed, peeled and cut into large cubes
2 oz of butter, 1/2 stick
3/4 cup of hot milk or cream,more or less as needed
Salt and pepper to taste

1. **Place potatoes in pot, covering with water and 2 tsp of salt. Cook until fork tender.**
2. **Heat milk and butter. It is very important to add hot milk not cold, makes all the difference.**
3. **Drain potatoes.**
4. **Beat cooked potatoes with a mixer (I like to use a potato ricer).**
5. **Slowly add hot milk and butter.**
6. **Salt and pepper to taste.**

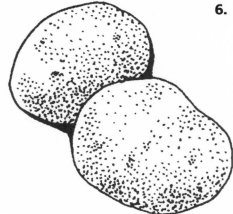

Wayne's hint ☞ My mother used a hand mixer to mash her potatoes. My grandmother used a ricer. I prefer the ricer and am very glad they are easy to find today. It makes for a smoother mashed potato with no lumps.

Tomato Green Beans

Tomato green beans is one of those non-baking recipes that uses cinnamon. I can guarantee, when you make this dish all of your guests will want to know what makes it so delicious. You can be honest, or you can lie like I have for years and tell them just garlic. But I don't usually lie. Well, I try not to lie. I'm always afraid that if I tell people the real secret ingredient, they'll stop eating. After writing this book, it looks like I'll have to start telling the truth.

Serves 4–6

1 lb of green beans, fresh or frozen
1 1/2 cups of whole tomatoes, hand crushed
2 cups of white potatoes, quartered
1 cup of onion, chopped
2 Tbsp of olive oil
2 tsp of garlic powder or fresh, chopped
1/4 tsp of crushed red pepper flakes
1 tsp of cinnamon
1 tsp of salt
1 tsp of pepper

1. **Place all ingredients in a mixing bowl. Blend well.**
2. **Pour mixture into a 9 x 13 baking dish.**
3. **Bake at 350 for approximately 11/2 hours or until potatoes are brown.**

Wayne's hint ☞ Try to get the potatoes to the top of the dish so they will brown nicely. Make sure they are well coated with sauce.

Honey Glazed Carrots

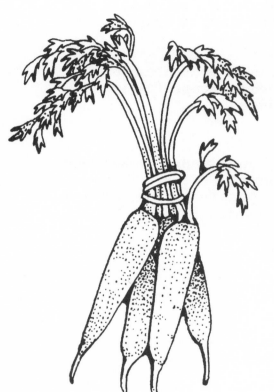

Serves 4–6

1 lb of carrots, peeled and cut into 1 inch slices
1/2 cup of onion, minced
2 oz of butter, 1/2 stick
2 Tbsp of honey
1/4 cup of pecans, chopped
Salt and pepper to taste

1. Place carrots in a pot and cover with water to 1 inch above.
2. Sauté onions in butter until soft.
3. Add honey and pecans to sautéed onions and simmer for 5 minutes.
4. When carrots have reached desired tenderness, drain.
5. Place carrots in a serving dish and cover with honey butter.
6. Salt and pepper and serve.

Wayne's hint ☞ I sometimes use baby carrots and steam them, leaving some of the green on for color.

Italian Green Peas ▪▪▪▪▪▪▪▪▪▪▪▪▪▪▪▪▪▪▪▪▪▪▪▪

Peas, to me, are better when frozen. For one thing, they are picked, shelled, and flash-frozen. Fresh peas do not stay sweet long. They begin to turn to starch and lose their flavor. I also do not like overcooked or canned peas. So, it's one of the few vegetables I prefer not to buy fresh.

Serves 4

1 lb of frozen green peas
1/2 cup of onion, finely chopped
2 oz of butter, 1/2 stick
2 Tbsp of olive oil
1/2 cup of Parmesan cheese, grated
1 tsp of garlic powder or fresh, chopped
1/2 cup of milk or half-and-half
Salt and pepper to taste

1. **Sauté onion and garlic in butter and oil for 3 minutes on medium heat.**
2. **Next, add peas. Sauté for another 3 minutes.**
3. **Then, add milk. Cook until peas reach your desired tenderness.**
4. **Place in a serving dish.**
5. **Top with grated Parmesan cheese and toss.**
6. **Adjust seasoning with salt and pepper.**
7. **Serve.**

Wayne's hint ☞ I like this dish with a lamb chop and a baked potato.

Roasted Potatoes ▪▪▪▪▪▪▪▪▪▪▪▪▪▪▪▪▪▪▪▪▪▪▪▪▪▪▪▪▪▪▪

My grandpa Targy lived in North Dakota with one of his many children, my Aunt Thordis. Those two were great company for me, a boy of five. Grandpa would play the fiddle and then show me his summer kitchen where he would bake bread and make blackberry pudding. Aunt Thordis would show me how to pump water from the well and store winter vegetables in the root cellar. She told me that the potatoes were always kept there in the winter to keep the floor warm.

One day, she was rocking me in Targy's rocking chair, all the while whispering Waynie, Waynie, Waynie. . . . My grandfather came in all excited and asked if I wanted to see jewels that came from the earth. I replied yes. We went out to the garden, where, with a pitchfork, he pierced the earth very deeply, rocked the pitchfork back and forth, and pushed down hard on the handle. Up came beautiful red potatoes. They sparkled in the sun and looked like rubies; they were jewels. Every time I cook red potatoes I think of this story, Targy and Thordis, and those sweet summer days.

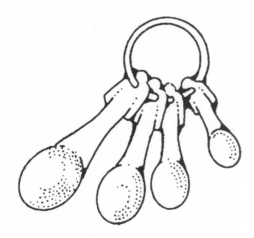

Serves 4

**3 lbs of cubed red potatoes, skins
on**
1 cup of red pepper, chopped
1 cup of onion, chopped
**1 Tbsp of fresh rosemary, remove
from stem**
**2 tsp of garlic powder or fresh,
crushed**
1/2 cup of olive oil
1 tsp of crushed red pepper flakes
2 Tbsp of fresh parsley, chopped
Paprika to taste
Salt and pepper to taste

1. **Wash, quarter and cube potatoes, leaving skins on.**
2. **Chop red pepper and onion, set aside.**
3. **Remove rosemary from stem, chop and set aside.**
4. **Combine olive oil, garlic, red pepper flakes and
   rosemary. Whisk and let stand for 15 minutes.
   Add salt and pepper.**
5. **In a bowl combine potatoes, red pepper, and
   onion.**
6. **Pour olive oil mixture over potatoes and toss like a
   salad. Let stand for 15–20 minutes.**
7. **Spread potatoes evenly on a large cookie sheet.
   Sprinkle with paprika and bake at 475 for 30
   minutes or until golden brown. Turn halfway
   through cooking.**
8. **Remove from oven and garnish with chopped, fresh
   parsley.**

 **Wayne's hint** ☞ I like using the left-overs for breakfast potatoes; served alongside
scrambled eggs and country sausage.

Wayne's Red Beans and Rice

Red beans and rice are served on Mondays, also known as washday in New Orleans. The lady of the house usually takes the ham bone from Sunday's meal along with red beans, covers them with water and spices and lets it simmer all day. She can get her laundry done and prepare a meal at the same time. The tradition of a simple meal on a particular day when chores are done also occurred in my family. That day was Saturday and our simple meal was hotdogs and beans.

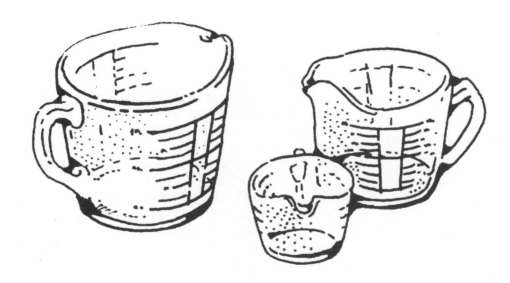

Serves 4–6

1 ham hock
1 lb of dry kidney or red beans
1 cup of celery, finely chopped
1 cup of onion, finely chopped
1 cup of green pepper, finely
  chopped
2 medium whole jalapeno
  peppers, minced or 2 tsp of
  cayenne pepper (use in place of
  jalapeno)
2 tsp of garlic powder or fresh,
  chopped
8 cups of water
2 bay leaves
2 tsp of thyme
1 tsp of cumin
1 tsp of cilantro
2 tsp of chicken bouillon granules
Salt and pepper to taste

1. **Rinse, sort and drain beans.**
2. **Let stand overnight or at least 4–6 hours, drain.**
3. **Beans soaked overnight will reduce cooking time. I usually eliminate this step and go for the extra cooking time that way I can be spontaneous with my cooking.**
4. **Add 8 cups of water and bouillon granules to drained beans.**
5. **Add ham hocks, onion, peppers, celery and jalapenos.**
6. **Add garlic, bay leaves, cumin, cilantro, thyme, salt and pepper.**
7. **Simmer beans until desired tenderness is reached, about 11/2–2hours.**
8. **Add water as needed to keep beans covered.**
9. **Serve over hot cooked rice and corn bread on the side.**

Wayne's hint ☞ I like to add precooked sausage to this mixture: andouille, Italian sweet, or kielbasa; cut into 1/2 inch slices. Also, I remove the meat from the ham hocks and add to the pot.

Wayne's Pickled Eggs with Red Beets

Pickled eggs go back to my Great Grandmother, Rose. Her daughter Helen, my grandmother, my mother, Rose, and my sister, Patricia, have continued the tradition. They serve them mostly at Easter, but I would be happy to have them at least once a week. The combination of beets and eggs is a great favorite of mine. As you can tell, I get very excited about most foods, except for turnips.

Makes 1/2 gallon

1 dozen eggs, hard-boiled and shelled
3–15 oz cans of medium whole red beets
1 1/2 cups of sugar
1 1/2 cups of white vinegar
2 Tbsp of pickling spice (wrapped in cheesecloth or in a tea ball)
1 cup of onion, chopped (I like the way the onions get pickled so I add twice the amount this recipe calls for.)
2 tsp of salt
1 tsp of ground red pepper

1. Place beets and juice in a large pot.
2. Add sugar, vinegar, red pepper, salt and pepper.
3. Next, add onions and pickling spice.
4. Bring to a simmer; allow to cook for 30 minutes. Remove from heat and add eggs.
5. Place in glass jar or large bowl and refrigerate for 24 hours.

Wayne's hint ☞ When shelling eggs, drain hot water from pot, smash eggs at sides of pot and run cold water over them. As you peel do so under running cold water; this will make the task easier.

Fried Red Tomatoes ▪▫▪▫▪▫▪▫▪▫▪▫▪▫▪▫▪▫▪▫▪▫▪▫

Most people in Maryland and the south fry green tomatoes. A friend of mine Larry taught me how to fry red ones. It's a favorite of mine in the summer when Maryland tomatoes are at their peak. Serve on white bread with mayonnaise, or as a side dish.

Serves 4–6

6 large tomatoes
1 cup of all-purpose flour
1 cup of cornmeal
2 Tbsp of sugar
Crisco enough to fry
Salt and pepper to taste

1. **Cut tomatoes in to 1/2–inch slices.**
2. **Mix flour, cornmeal, sugar, salt and pepper into a bowl for dredging.**
3. **Place tomatoes into dry mixture, turn and pat.**
4. **Heat oil in a skillet.**
5. **Place tomatoes in skillet and brown on each side.**
6. **Remove to a paper towel to drain.**

Wayne's hint ☞ This recipe can be easily adapted to use green tomatoes. Crisco is the best shortening to use to fry.

Zucchini Casserole with Cheddar Cheese ▪▫▪▫▪▫▪▫▪▫▪▫▪▫▪

My mother often boiled potatoes. When they were tender she would drain off the water and add enough milk to cover them. Then, she would add salt and pepper along with a generous amount of fresh parsley. Whenever I am stumped for a side dish that calls for a starch, I can rely on parsley potatoes—they're always wonderful. But it's zucchini we're supposed to be talking about here! There never seems to be enough recipes that call for zucchini, a very versatile squash. You can rely this one, it's one of my trusted favorites.

Serves 4–6

2 cups of zucchini, 1/4 inch slices
1 cup of onion, chopped
1 cup of fennel
1 1/2 cups of tomatoes, fresh or can, chopped
1 tsp of basil, dried
1 tsp of garlic powder or fresh, chopped
1 tsp of thyme, dried
1 tsp of marjoram, dried
1 tsp of rosemary, dried
1/2 tsp of red pepper flakes
2 cups of cheddar cheese, shredded
2 tsp of salt

1. Assemble all vegetables in a large bowl.
2. Next, add basil, garlic, thyme, rosemary, marjoram, salt and red pepper flakes.
3. Toss like a salad and let stand for 15 minutes.
4. Then, in an 11x7 or medium baking dish place vegetables.
5. Top casserole with cheese.
6. Bake at 350 for about 60 minutes or until zucchini is fork tender.

Wayne's hint ☞ This recipe is wonderful served as a side dish. I often serve it with baked halibut and boiled parsley potatoes.

Roasted Vegetables

Serves 6–8

2 cups of sweet potato, peeled and cubed
2 cups of fennel, cut into cubes
2 cups of eggplant, cut into cubes, skin-on
2 cups of white potatoes, cubed
1 cup of carrot, 1–inch slices
2 cups of onion, quartered
2 cups of red pepper, cubed
1 tsp of crushed red pepper flakes
Dressing
1/2 cup of olive oil
2 tsp of garlic powder or fresh, chopped
1 Tbsp of rosemary, dried or fresh, chopped
2 tsp of salt
2 tsp of pepper

1. Prepare all vegetables and place in large bowl.
2. Mix dressing and whisk until smooth, then let stand for 15 minutes.
3. Pour dressing over vegetables and toss. Let stand 15 minutes.
4. Place coated vegetables on a baking sheet. Make sure vegetables are spread evenly on pan so all sides can brown.
5. Roast at 475 for 30 minutes or until vegetables are tender and golden brown.

Wayne's hint ☞ You can use any of your favorite vegetables in this recipe. Try using acorn squash, rutabagas, turnips, or asparagus.

Wayne's Kielbasa and Sauerkraut

Kielbasa and sauerkraut was served at every holiday meal that my grandmother and mother ever prepared. Baltimore's strong German and Polish heritage has made it a favorite in many households, regardless of their nationality. This dish is a great idea for Oktoberfest.

Serves 4

1 lb of kielbasa
2 lb bag of sauerkraut
1 cup of apple of your choice, chopped
1 Tbsp of brown sugar
1 tsp of caraway seed
1 tsp of celery seed
1 tsp of coriander
1 tsp of fennel seed
2 cups of chicken stock or 2 cups of water with 2 tsp of chicken bouillon granules
Salt and pepper to taste

1. Wash sauerkraut and drain. Set aside.
2. Bring chicken stock to a boil in a medium size pot.
3. Next, add sauerkraut, apples, caraway, brown sugar, celery seed, coriander, fennel seed, salt and pepper.
4. Add kielbasa and cook for another 45 minutes.

For Pork Roast
1. Place roast on top of bed of kraut.
2. Brush pork with olive oil, garlic powder and salt and pepper.
3. Cover and place in oven at 350 until pork is done.

Wayne's hint ☞ Kielbasa contains a large amount of garlic that will permeate your refrigerator, so remember to keep it tightly sealed.

Scalloped Sweet Potatoes with Apples

Every year for the last twenty-five years I have received the same invitation from a friend of mine Mary Della Davis. Once we were neighbors, but then I moved away. Even if we haven't had much contact throughout the rest of the year, I still get an invitation to Thanksgiving dinner. When I ask if I can bring anything, she always responds, "You can bring those sweet potatoes and apples." Sometimes I play around and don't offer to bring anything. Inevitably, there's a pause and then Mary, in her sweet, whiny voice says, "would you mind bringing those sweet potatoes and apples?" I laugh and say sure. I never quite know if it's me or the sweet potatoes and apples that gets the invite.

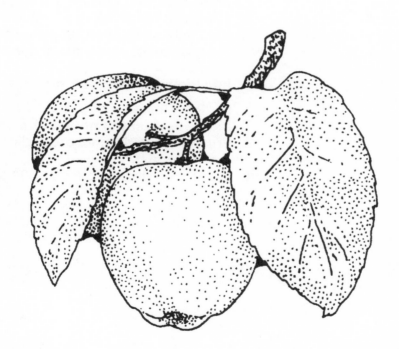

Serves 4–6

2 large sweet potatoes
3 large granny smith apples, cored, peeled and thinly
   sliced
1 cup of bread crumbs
1 cup of maple syrup
4 oz of butter, 1 stick
1/2 cup of pecans, chopped
1/2 cup of golden raisins
1/2 tsp of cinnamon

1. Peel and cook sweet potatoes until almost done. Don't
   over cook.
2. Cool potatoes and cut into 1/2 inch slices. Core and
   slice granny smith apple (or any tart variety).
3. In a greased baking dish, layer with sweet potatoes
   then apples, raisins, nuts, pats of butter, dash of
   cinnamon and sprinkled breadcrumbs.
4. Alternate layers to the top of dish.
5. Pour syrup over top and dot with pats of butter.
6. Cover with foil and bake at 375 until apples are done,
   about 45 minutes.

Wayne's hint ☞ I like using Granny Smith or any tart variety of apples; but if I had my choice, I would go for a Winesap.

Scalloped Potatoes with Smithfield Ham ▪▪▪▪▪▪▪▪

My dear friend Kate inspired this dish. She once told me she was served this dish at a friend's house in New York. I replicated it by using my mother's recipe for scalloped potatoes to which I added Smithfield ham and cheese. My mother would always prepare scalloped potatoes when she was in a mood to please my father, and we could always tell when an argument was over when we had scalloped potatoes. I thought of it as redemption food. Needless to say, we didn't have them often.

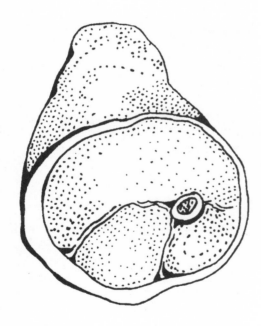

Serves 4–6

4 oz of Smithfield ham (also known as country ham, cut
   into bite size pieces
2 lbs of peeled potatoes, thinly sliced
1 cup of onion, finely chopped
1/2 cup of flour
2 oz of butter, 1/2 stick
2 1/4 cups of milk or half-and-half
3 cups of Swiss cheese, shredded
Nutmeg, dash each layer
Salt and pepper to taste

1. Grease an 8x8, 2–inch deep casserole dish.
2. Remember you will have three layers of potatoes, ham
   and cheese, so be prepared to divide equally.
3. Layer bottom of dish with potatoes.
4. Dust potatoes with flour and top with 5 pats of butter.
5. Next, add ham, Swiss cheese, onion, nutmeg, salt and
   pepper.
6. Cover first layer with milk until it's visible between
   potato slices.
7. Repeat layering steps until dish is filled and covered
   with milk.
8. Final layer should be Swiss cheese, pats of butter,
   nutmeg, salt and pepper.
9. Bake in 350 oven for 1 hour or until golden brown and
   potatoes fork tender.

Wayne's hint ☞ Country ham or Smithfield ham is very salty. Make sure you are careful
with the amount and size of ham pieces you use. You want the flavor of the ham, not the
saltiness.

Apple Butter Beans ▪▫▪▫▪▫▪▫▪▫▪▫▪▫▪▫▪▫▪▫▪▫▪▫▪▫▪

I love beans. I often cook this dish as an entrée—it makes a whole meal. I often cook a pound of sausage, Italian sweet or Kielbasa, cut it into 1/2" slices and add it to this recipe. A nice salad and some crusty bread and there's your meal. For dessert I like serving poached pears with a large dollop of ginger-flavored whipped cream.

Serves 4–6

16 oz bag of large dried lima
  beans (baby lima beans or navy
  beans can also be used)
1 cup of chopped celery
1 Tbsp of garlic powder or fresh,
  chopped
8 oz of lean bacon cut in 2–inch
  pieces
2 cups of cold water or chicken
  stock
Sauce
3/4 cup of ketchup
3 Tbsp of apple butter
2 Tbsp of yellow mustard
1 Tbsp of Worcestershire sauce
1/4 tsp of ground red pepper
1/2 tsp of ground cloves
1 tsp garlic powder or fresh,
  chopped
1/2 tsp of ground ginger
1/2 tsp of horseradish
1/2 tsp of thyme

1. Soak beans overnight making sure they are covered
   with 2" of water.
2. In this recipe, I think it is important to soak your
   beans overnight.
3. In a pot, sauté bacon.
4. Drain excess fat (leaving approximately 2 Tbsp of
   drippings), add the onions, celery and garlic and
   sauté until translucent.
5. Drain the beans and add them to the bacon, onions
   and garlic.
6. Stir ingredients together, cover and allow them to
   sweat for 5 minutes (this will allow the beans to
   absorb the flavors of the bacon, onion, and
   garlic).
7. In a mixing bowl, combine sauce ingredients
   (making sure to mix thoroughly). Set aside.
8. Add 2 cups of cold water (or chicken stock) to the
   beans, bring to a boil then reduce to a simmer
   and allow to cook for a half hour.
9. Once the beans have cooked for 1/2 hour
   thoroughly mix in the sauce.
10. Cook until beans are tender, stirring occasionally
    (for 1/2 hour to 45 minutes)

Wayne's hint ☞ You can also transfer to a baking dish, top with hot dogs, and baked at
350 for 15–20 minutes.

Eva's Welsh Rarebit with Broccoli

Nathan helped me edit this book. Eva is Nathan's grandmother. As Nathan tells it, Eva might call just about anything Welsh Rarebit if she doesn't know what else to call it. This recipe is for her.

Serves 4
1 lb of broccoli, fresh or frozen
1 cup of fresh tomato, chopped
1/2 lb (approximately 1/2 cup) of bacon, cut into
    1/2–inch slices then cooked
Welsh Rarebit
1 cup of grated cheddar cheese
1/2 cup of half-and-half
1 Tbsp of butter
1/2 tsp of salt
1/4 tsp of dry mustard
1 tsp of Worcestershire sauce

1. Steam broccoli until desired tenderness.
2. Drain broccoli and place in a serving dish.
3. On low heat melt butter. Add half-and-half and cheese.
    Allow cheese to melt.
4. Stir constantly until well blended.
5. Add salt, dry mustard and Worcestershire sauce, blend,
    then remove from heat.
6. Pour Welsh rarebit over broccoli.
7. Top with tomato and chopped bacon then serve.

Wayne's hint ☞ This tastes so good, I double the amount of rarebit and leave the same amount of broccoli.

Sautéed Mushrooms with Blue Cheese and Walnuts ▞▞▞▞

Serves 4

1 lb of white mushrooms, sliced
1/2 cup of finely chopped white onion
1 cup of walnut pieces
4 oz of bleu cheese, crumbled (Stilton or
  Gorgonzola)
1 tsp of garlic powder or fresh, chopped
3 Tbsp of olive oil (or as needed)
1 Tbsp of butter
Salt and pepper to taste

1. In a large skillet, melt butter with the olive oil
2. Add in walnuts and sauté for approximately 3
   minutes.
3. Add onion and garlic; sauté until tender (not
   brown).
4. Add mushrooms and cook until they are lightly
   brown.
5. Transfer to a serving dish and add the crumbled
   bleu cheese on top.

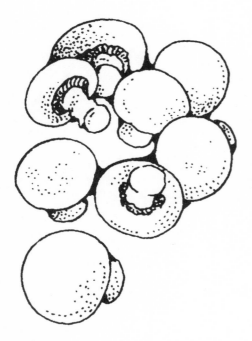

Wayne's hint ☞ I like to vary this recipe with a combination of white and wild mushrooms like Morels and Portobellos.

Creamed Spinach ▓▒▓▒▓▒▓▒▓▒▓▒▓▒▓▒▓▒▓▒▓▒▓▒

Serves 4

1 lb of spinach, frozen and cut
1/4 cup of butter
1/4 cup of flour
1/2 cup of onion, finely chopped
1/2 tsp of garlic powder or fresh, chopped
1/4 tsp of ground red pepper flakes
1/4 tsp of nutmeg
2 cups of milk

1. In butter, sauté onions and garlic.
2. Next, add flour. Allow to cook for 3 minutes.
3. Add nutmeg and red pepper flakes.
4. Bring to a boil and slowly add milk. Allow to thicken.
5. Then, add spinach and reduce heat.
6. If the sauce is at the desired consistency, serve. If it is too thick then add more milk at this time.

Wayne's hint ☞ I like keeping several bags of spinach in my freezer so I can make this recipe anytime I want to.

Desserts

Apple Crisp ▪▨▪▨▪▨▪▨▪▨▪▨▪▨▪▨▪▨▪▨▪▨▪▨▪▨▪▨▪▨▪▨▪

You can make this recipe in a matter of minutes. The reward is the aroma that wafts through your home and alerts your family to this wonderful homemade dessert. It is also good idea to prepare it if you're trying to sell your home. Just imagine someone walking in and saying, "Ooh, this smells good. I think I want to buy this house."

Serves 4

6 cups tart apples (about 6 apples)
2 Tbsp of lemon juice
1/2 cup of all-purpose flour
1/2 cup of packed brown sugar
1 tsp of cinnamon
4 oz of salted butter, 1 stick
A dash of nutmeg

1. **Preheat oven to 375.**
2. **Pare apples. Core and cut into 1/2 inch wedges then cut wedges in half crosswise.**
3. **Place apples in a 7x11 pie-pan or baking dish.**
4. **Sprinkle lemon juice over apples.**

Making the Crumble
1. **In a mixing bowl, lightly work flour, sugar, cinnamon, nutmeg and butter into a crumble (do not allow to become oily).**
2. **Spread crumble over the apples and bake in the oven for 30 to 45 minutes or until apples are fork tender.**

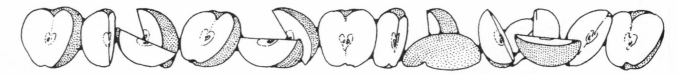

Wayne's hint ☞ Dried cranberries or cherries can be added to the apples. Soak berries, 1 cup, in warm water for 10 minutes, drain and pat dry. Then add to apples before placing in baking dish. You can also add 1/2 cup chopped walnuts.

Wayne's Chocolate Brownie ▪▪▪▪▪▪▪▪▪▪▪▪▪▪▪▪▪▪

This recipe has been used in the restaurant since the first days of The Soup Kitchen Ltd more than twenty-five years ago. Dena Napoli, a newscaster and food journalist at a local NBC station once said, "These are the best brownies I have ever eaten."

Serves 4–6

12 oz of chocolate
3/4 cup of butter
4 eggs
1 cup of sugar
2 tsp of vanilla
1 cup of flour
2 tsp of baking powder
1/2 tsp of salt
1/2 cup of walnuts, chopped

1. **Melt together chocolate and butter. Set aside.**
2. **Next, with a mixer, blend eggs, sugar and vanilla, mixing well.**
3. **Sift together flour, baking powder and salt.**
4. **Gradually add dry ingredients to eggs and sugar.**
5. **Then, add melted chocolate and butter, making sure mixture is not too hot.**
6. **Grease an 11x7 pan and dust with cocoa. Pour into a baking dish.**
7. **Sprinkle walnuts over mixture once in pan.**
8. **Bake at 350 for 25 minutes.**

Wayne's hint ☞ Remember, never overbake brownies if you want them to stay moist, and always use the best available chocolate.

Mashed Potato Easter Eggs

When I was a boy I looked forward every year to these wonderful Easter eggs. My favorite was the one made with coconut. Grandmother Helen would always remember my favorite and set them aside just for me. If you care to enjoy my favorite, all you have to do is add 1/2 cup flaked coconut during the kneading process. It's surprising how the potato in this recipe tones down the sweetness so the Easter egg is not over-rich.

1/4 lb of butter or margarine, softened
2 lb of confectioners sugar, sifted
1/2 cup of potatoes
1 1/2 tsp of vanilla
1/2 lb of bitter chocolate

1. Peel, then boil potatoes in salt water until soft, then drain.
2. Mash potatoes and allow them to cool.
3. Blend butter and potatoes.
4. Add sugar and vanilla to potato mixture.
5. Knead mixture by hand until creamy. Mold into egg shape.
6. Place in refrigerator and chill for one hour.
7. Next, melt chocolate in double boiler. Then allow chocolate to cool a bit.
8. Dip chilled eggs in chocolate and drain on wire rack.
9. Then, place on waxed paper and return to refrigerator to harden.

Wayne's hint ☞ This is the one thing I always forget to do. To place the egg in the refrigerator before dipping it into the chocolate. Please learn from my mistakes. It makes for a mess.

Grandma Philyaw's Bourbon Sweet Potato Pie ▪▪▪▪▪▪▪

Christopher Philyaw, whose grandmother would often visit him while he was working at the restaurant, gave this recipe to me. I've made her recipe on TV as well as at home many times. Both family and friends enjoy this wonderful pie and it's a nice change from pumpkin pie.

2 cups of sweet potatoes
1/4 cup of butter
3 eggs
1 cup of milk
1 1/4 tsp of salt
1/4 tsp of nutmeg
1 tsp of vanilla
1/4 cup of bourbon
1 unbaked 9" pie shell

1. **Cook sweet potatoes, mash and let cool.**
2. **Add butter.**
3. **Mix together eggs, milk, salt, vanilla, nutmeg and bourbon.**
4. **Combine sweet potatoes and egg mixture and blend well.**
5. **Pour into pie shell.**
6. **Bake at 450 for the first 15 minutes.**
7. **Then turn temperature down to 350 and bake for about 1 hour and 20 minutes or until inserted knife comes out clean.**

Wayne's hint ☞ You can prepare this recipe without the crust. It makes for a wonderful pudding.

Christmas Bread Pudding

For years I've tried to come up with the perfect recipe for bread pudding. Once when I had an abundance of potato rolls, I decided to experiment once more with bread pudding. To my surprise, it came out perfectly. I loved it and decided to do it for my TV audience. Everyone loved the recipe just as much as I did; in fact I have proof (don't you doubt me). A viewer wrote: "Dear Wayne, for years I have searched for the perfect bread pudding recipe. I found it when I tried your recipe as demonstrated on TV. I can die a happy woman!" Signed Bernie Meadocrouft. I hope I got the name right. Her signature was hard to read but her appreciation wasn't. I love her even though I don't know her. This dish may say "Christmas," but if you want it in July, you can have it in July.

12 cups of bread cubes (potato rolls work best)
2 cups of sugar
8 eggs
2 quarts of half-and-half
1/2 tsp of salt
1 Tbsp of vanilla
16 oz of candied fruit or 1 cup of raisins (I like the golden.)
1 Tbsp of butter

1. Place bread cubes in large mixing bowl.
2. In a separate bowl, mix together half-and-half and sugar.
3. Add eggs and blend thoroughly.
4. Add salt and vanilla.
5. Add candied fruit and mix thoroughly.
6. Pour egg and fruit mix over bread cubes.
7. Let stand for one to two hours.
8. Butter a 9 1/2 x 13 1/2, 2–inch deep baking dish.
9. Spoon mixture into baking pan.
10. Bake at 350 for 1 to 1 1/2 hours or until golden brown.

Wayne's hint ☞ Recipe can be cut in half to accommodate your needs. Please don't look at this just for Christmas. Omit the candy, fruit, and raisins, if you like. This is a wonderful bread pudding.

Pumpkin Custard with Pecan Caramel Glaze ▪️▫️▪️▫️▪️▫️▪️

It was a cold winter day in January that to me felt like Thanksgiving. I wanted pumpkin pie. I had the pumpkin, but didn't feel like making a piecrust (which I'm no good at anyway). So, I took a little of this and a little of that and—voila! This recipe was born. I loved it so much I ate it all in one day. It called my name. It wouldn't leave me alone. If I went upstairs to take a nap, the pumpkin custard would call, "Wayne." I would go down, take just a little bite and resume my nap. When I woke up, it said, "Wayne, just a little bit more." It called my name throughout the day, which happened while reading the newspaper, and while watching *The Godfather III* (my favorite). Finally the last call, "there's only a little bite left, Wayne." That was all the justification I needed to finish off the whole wonderful dessert. To this day I don't feel guilty for answering the call. I was a good soldier.

Serves 4–6

Custard
16 oz can of pumpkin
14 oz can of sweetened condensed milk
2 whole eggs
2 egg yolks
1/4 tsp of nutmeg
1/4 tsp of cinnamon
1/4 tsp of ginger
1/2 cup of half-and-half

Glaze
1/2 cup of brown sugar
1/2 cup of butter
2 Tbsp of cream
4–8 oz of pecans (or walnuts), whole or chopped

Making the Custard
1. **Place pumpkin in mixing bowl and mix in cinnamon, nutmeg, ginger, add whole eggs and yolks, condensed milk and half-and-half.**
2. **Transfer the mix into a greased baking dish.**
Bake at 350 for about 1 hour.

Making the Glaze
1. **Melt butter in the pan, then add in the brown sugar and let bubble for 3 minutes on a medium heat, and then add cream.**
2. **Pour the glaze over the custard and garnish with nuts.**

Wayne's hint ☞ I always use canned pumpkin. I find cooking my own pumpkin or even roasting it doesn't have an intense flavor as the canned.

Peppermint Bark

I once needed a recipe for a holiday dessert. I was stumped when Nathan, who worked at the restaurant, came to my rescue by telling me about a candy his mother would make using candy canes and white chocolate. That was enough to get me excited about creating this recipe.

2 lb of white chocolate
12 candy canes

1. Place candy canes in a plastic bag and hammer in to 1/4–inch chunks (or smaller).
2. Melt the chocolate in a double boiler or place a bowl atop a pot of boiling water.
3. Combine candy cane pieces with melted chocolate.
4. Line cookie sheet with parchment or wax paper.
5. Pour mixture on to cookie sheet and place in fridge for 45 minutes to 1 hour (until firm).
6. Remove from cookie pan and break in to chips (like peanut brittle).

Wayne's hint ☞ 2 cups of cashews or any of your favorite nuts can be used instead of the candy canes.

Aunt Charlotte's Cold Oven Cake

Every time my Aunt Charlotte would come to my house I would ask her to bring this cake. Actually, she would always bring it anyway, even if I forgot to ask. I never threatened to stop inviting her, she always brought it because she liked me and knew I loved her cake. Now, you have to understand that whenever I invite someone to my house I never ask him or her to bring anything. I would say, this is the only request I have ever made in this regard. It's just that I love this cake so much—as much as my Aunt Charlotte, who, by the way, is my mother's sister. Aunt Charlotte's the pretty one. I know my mother will get mad at me saying that. Oh well.

3 cups of sugar
1/2 lb of butter, softened
7 eggs
3 cups of cake flour, sifted twice
1 cup of whipping cream
2 tsp of vanilla extracct

Coconut Frosting
2 cups of coconut
1 lb of confectioners 10–X sugar
1/2 cup butter or margarine, softened
1 tsp of vanilla extract
3 Tbsp of milk

1. **Butter and flour a 10–inch tube pan.**
2. **Next, thoroughly cream together sugar and butter.**
3. **Add eggs, one at a time, beating well after each addition.**
4. **Mix in half the flour.**
5. **Next, add the whipping cream.**
6. **Then add the other half of the flour.**
7. **Add vanilla.**
8. **Now, pour batter into prepared pan.**
9. **Set in cold oven and turn heat to 350.**
10. **Bake for one hour to 70 minutes (until a sharp knife inserted in cake comes out clean).**
11. **Cool in pan for five minutes.**
12. **In a large bowl, beat together sugar, butter, vanilla and add milk until smooth.**
13. **If necessary, add more milk until frosting is spreading consistency.**
14. **Frost cake and sprinkle coconut.**

Wayne's hint ☞ Unless you're prepared to eat the whole thing, invite friends over. I found this out the hard way.

Banana Cake

This banana cake, along with several other desserts, was created at The Soup Kitchen, Ltd. by an industrious and creative young woman named Sandy. She had once worked for a German baker. Many of her recipes had a richness and heartiness that I believe came with her background. In other words, neither she nor her recipes were fancy or fluffy in texture or design. Simplicity with good ingredients was her hallmark, which is the way it is to this day at the restaurant. Sandy left after several years, leaving behind her high standard for preparing desserts. She left to become an actor. I haven't seen her on a TV show, in a movie, or on Broadway. And I can't remember her last name or where she moved to in California. I think of her as my dessert angel. She came, she baked, and then she left. May her fondest dream come true. Thanks, Sandy.

1 1/2 cups of margarine, room
  temperature
3 cups of sugar
5 whole eggs, room temperature
3 whole bananas, mashed
4 cups of flour
2 tsp of baking soda
1 tsp baking powder
1 1/2 cups of buttermilk (or sour
  milk)
1 1/2 tsp of vanilla extract

Banana Frosting
1 banana, smashed
1 lb of confectioners 10–X sugar
1/2 cup of butter or margarine,
  softened
1 tsp of vanilla extract
3 Tbsp of milk

1. In a mixing bowl, stir together margarine and sugar until fluffy. This is very important, most people do not beat long enough so air can get into the mixture allowing cake to rise properly.
2. Slowly add eggs and bananas to mixture.
3. In a separate mixing bowl, combine flour, baking soda and baking powder.
4. Combine the two mixtures together.
5. Next, add vanilla. Then slowly add milk. Continue beating until mixture is light and fluffy.
6. Grease and then dust two 9–inch cake pans, 2–inch deep with flour.
7. Pour cake mixture evenly into pans.
8. Bake at 350 for 40 minutes (until cake moves from side of pan).
9. In a large bowl, beat together sugar, butter, banana, vanilla and milk until smooth.
10. If necessary, add more milk until frosting is spreading consistency.
11. Once cake is cooled frost cake.

Wayne's hint ☞ Frosting with fresh banana has a tendency to turn brown. Try to serve this cake on the same day you frost it.

Banana Bavarian Crème Cake ▪▪▪▪▪▪▪▪▪▪▪▪▪▪▪▪

This cake uses one layer of the two that are required for my banana cake recipe. The recipe for Bavarian Crème is enough for the two layers. Please, when making one cake, which happens to be one layer, only use half the Bavarian Crème when adding it to your one pint of whipped cream.

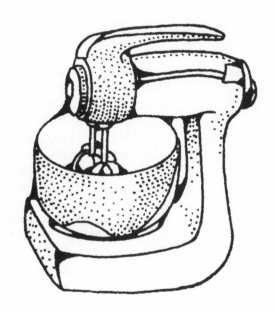

1 quart of scalding milk
6 egg yolks
1 cup of sugar
1 Tbsp of gelatin
2 pints of whipping cream
1 cup of walnuts, finely chopped
2 ripe bananas

1. Make the cake using the banana cake recipe.
2. Whip together egg yolks, sugar and gelatin.
3. In the pot of scalding milk, slowly fold in egg mix.
4. Simmer over a low heat for 10–15 minutes.
5. Transfer to a large mixing bowl. Cool to room temperature and then refrigerate for approximately 2 hours or until mix is firm.
6. In a mixing bowl, whip 1 pint of whipping cream in to peaks (be careful not to overwhip.)
7. Fold whipped cream and custard mix together.
8. Whip second pint of whipping cream into peaks.
9. Cut one layer of cake lengthwise, setting the top aside.
10. Cover the bottom half with Bavarian crème.
11. Thinly slice the two bananas and layer them on top of the Bavarian crème.
12. Place top of cake on bottom half and frost the entire cake with the second pint of whipped cream.
13. Once cake is frosted, dust the sides of the frosted cake with chopped walnuts.

Wayne's hint ☞ When making this Bavarian Crème, you can half the recipe because it makes a lot. I don't half it because I enjoy eating it as a pudding with fresh fruit.

Peach Cobbler: 1 Cup, 1 Cup, 1 Cup, 2

Susan Martin, who used to work at the restaurant gave this recipe to me. It was from her grandmother, who was from the south. Over the years, I have talked to many women customers from Georgia, North and South Carolina, and Alabama. They all know this recipe. Someone, somewhere, a long time ago in the deep south came up with the simplest way to make cobbler. Oh, is this good. Try saying the name of this recipe without singing.

1 cup of sugar
1 cup of self-rising flour
1 cup of milk
2 cups of peaches (6 or 7 peaches or 1–32 oz can)
4 oz of margarine, 1 stick

1. Preheat oven to 350 degrees.
2. Peel peaches and cut into wedges. Place peaches in a pot and cover with water.
3. Next, add 1/2 cup of sugar. Simmer until peaches are fork tender, not soft.
4. In a round, 2-quart bowl, add margarine and place in oven. Allow it to melt and the dish to become hot.
5. In a mixing bowl, add milk, flour, and remaining sugar. Blend into a batter.
6. Remove dish from oven and swirl melted margarine in dish to coat all sides.
7. Pour in batter.
8. With a slotted spoon, add peaches in the center of the bowl. Gently pour in 1/2 cup of the syrup. Do not go to the rim of the bowl. Cobbler will run over during baking.
9. Place in 350 oven and bake for one hour.
10. Serve hot topped with ice cream.

Wayne's hint ☞ Any canned or fresh fruit may be used. Do not use pie filling.

Carrot Cake

This is one of those recipes that Sandy brought to The Soup Kitchen, Ltd.

4 cups of carrots, shredded
3 cups of sugar
3 cups of flour
2 cups of oil
1 Tbsp of vanilla
6 eggs
2 tsp of baking soda
11/2 tsp of cinnamon
1/2 tsp of nutmeg
1/2 tsp of cloves
1 1/2 tsp of salt

Frosting
16 oz of cream cheese, softened
1 cup of butter
2 cups of confectioners sugar
1 tsp of vanilla or lemon
Dash of salt

1. In a bowl, mix together sugar and oil.
2. Add eggs and vanilla. Set aside.
3. In a separate bowl, mix together flour, baking soda, salt, cinnamon, nutmeg and cloves.
4. Next, mix all ingredients together adding carrots.
5. Grease and dust two 9–inch cake pans with flour.
6. Pour mixture into pans and bake at 400 until cake moves from side of pan.
7. In a bowl blend together cream cheese and butter. Be sure to mix well.
8. Add sugar, vanilla and salt.
9. Beat until light and fluffy.
10. Spread onto cooled cake.

Wayne's hint ☞ I sometimes don't frost this cake. Yvette and I will use one layer cut into wedges as a breakfast cake. All it needs is a Caramel Macchiato from Starbucks.

Grandmother's Christmas Jell-O

I am so happy to put in print for my older brother, Keith, that this is Grandmother's recipe. He constantly refers to this dessert as one he remembers originating in North Dakota where my father was from. I don't know if Keith believes what he is saying or if he just likes causing trouble. I think it's the latter. It sure stirs up a lot of arguments that end in hysterical laughter. Somebody yells: "It's Grandmother's." Keith laughingly defends his position by saying, "No, it's North Dakota Jell-O." Everyone argues with him. He has no one on his side. Why do families do this? I don't know, but I'm sure we're not the only ones who argue over silly things. For once and for all, for family or friends, THIS IS MY GRANDMOTHER'S RECIPE! Thank you.

1– 3 oz package of lemon Jell-O
2– 3 oz packages of lime Jell-O
1– 12 oz can of evaporated milk
6 oz of cream cheese, softened (6 oz packages of cream cheese are not sold in the store so you will need to buy two 3 oz packages.)
1 can of crushed pineapple, drained

1. Prepare lime Jell-O according to instructions on the package.
2. Place in the refrigerator and allow to slightly thicken, about 1 hour.
3. Mix in pineapple and place back into refrigerator.
4. Next, make lemon Jell-O according to instructions on the package.
5. Place in refrigerator and allow to slightly thicken.
6. Then, whip cream cheese and milk with lemon Jell-O.
7. Being sure lime Jell-O is completely set, pour lemon Jell-O mixture over top.
8. Refrigerate until all ingredients are completely firm.

Wayne's hint ☞ Even if you mess up this recipe it will still taste great!

Shenandoah Apple Cake

This is another one of Sandy's recipes. It won the award for Maryland's best apple cake. I think it was either *Baltimore Magazine* or *The City Paper* that bestowed this honor. Usually a category would have several nominees. There was no category and no other nominees. So, whoever the judge was, loved this cake and created a category in order to give it an award. Whoever you are, we thank you.

3 cups of apples, peeled
3 cups of sugar
3 cups of flour
6 eggs
1 1/2 cups of oil
2 tsp of baking soda
1 tsp of salt
1 tsp of cinnamon
1/2 tsp of nutmeg
1 cup of walnuts, chopped
2 tsp of vanilla

Glaze
1 cup of brown sugar
1/2 cup of butter
1/4 cup of cream

1. Mix together sugar and oil.
2. Next, add eggs.
3. In a separate bowl, mix flour, baking soda, salt, cinnamon, nutmeg and walnuts.
4. Next, combine the two mixtures together.
5. Toss together apples and vanilla.
6. Fold apples into mixture.
7. Grease and dust two cake pans. Bake at 400 until cake moves from side of pan.
8. Melt butter in a pan then add brown sugar. Bring to a boil, then add cream.
9. Cook for 3 minutes.
10. Pour over top of cooled cake.
11. Garnish with chopped walnuts on top.

Wayne's hint ☞ When making the caramel topping for this cake, remember to cook for only 3 minutes. Any longer, it will turn hard.

Peaches and Cream Trifle

3 cups of peaches, fresh
6 cups of pound cake, broken into large pieces
1/2 cup of brandy
3 cups of pudding or tapioca
3 cups of whipped cream or non-dairy Cool Whip
   (can be sweetened with powdered sugar or
   honey)
1 Tbsp of sugar

1. Peel and slice peaches.
2. Next, sprinkle sugar over peaches and toss.
3. Add brandy and toss again.
4. Let stand for about 20 minutes.
5. Place a layer of pound cake on the bottom of a
   large bowl.
6. Next, add a layer of peaches.
7. Then, a layer of pudding or tapioca.
8. Repeat steps 5, 6 and 7 until you reach the top of
   the bowl.
9. Top with whipped cream.
10. Chill for about 30 minutes and serve.

Wayne's hint ☞ In Maryland, August is the best time to buy peaches. I prefer not using canned. It's nice to have a dish that's seasonal.

Grandma's Macaroons

These were my favorite cookies when I was a little boy. I don't remember what my grandmother did for my siblings as far as baking. I believe she was an honorable woman who divided things equally. However, I would always have a tin set-aside just for me filled with macaroons. She made me feel very special. We all need someone to make us feel that way.

Makes six cookies

1 1/2 cup of coconut
1/2 cup of sugar
2 Tbsp of flour
1/2 tsp of almond extract
1/2 tsp of salt
2 egg whites

1. **In a bowl, combine coconut, sugar, flour and salt.**
2. **Stir in unbeaten egg whites and almond extract. Mix well.**
3. **Drop, by teaspoon, onto lightly greased baking sheet.**
4. **Bake at 325 for 20–25 minutes or until edges are brown.**
5. **Remove from baking sheet immediately.**

Wayne's hint ☞ I like dipping these macaroons half way into melted chocolate.

Hot Fudge

This hot fudge is the best and I almost lost the recipe. You know how you sometimes do a recipe over and over again and you think you'll never forget it? Well, wait a couple of years and then see if you remember. I didn't. I was known for my fudge sauce. The only other place in town that could come close was Marconie's, and customers would constantly argue over which one they thought was the best. Now you have my secret for making hot fudge. You won't get theirs. So, I win.

1 lb of chocolate
1 quart of half-and-half
1 cup of sugar
1/2 cup of brown sugar
2 oz of butter, 1/2 stick
1/4 cup of rum

1. On low heat or in a double-broiler melt butter and chocolate together.
2. Stir in sugar and rum. Then, slowly add half-and-half.
2. Once fudge cools it may be refrigerated and then reheated in microwave before serving.

Wayne's hint ☞ Serve this over ice cream, or pound cake. Even a large Tablespoon in a cold glass of milk makes wonderful use of this glorious sauce.

Rum Pumpkin Pie

Pie Crust
1 cup of all-purpose flour
1/2 tsp of salt
3/8 cup of Crisco shortening
2 1/2 Tbsp of cold water

Filling
2 eggs
29 oz can of pumpkin pie mix
2/3 cup of evaporated milk
1 Tbsp of dark rum
1/2 cup of coconut flakes

Making the Crust
1. Preheat oven to 425.
2. In a mixing bowl, combine flour and salt. Then, slowly cut in the shortening.
3. Sprinkle in the water and knead the mix to a ball.
4. Place in refrigerator and allow to chill for at least 30 minutes.
5. Flatten the dough into a pancake and roll it out to fit your 9–inch pie pan.

Making the Filling
6. In a large bowl, beat eggs lightly then stir in pumpkin pie mix, evaporated milk and dark rum.
7. Place filling in pie pan and sprinkle coconut on top.
8. Bake in oven for 15 minutes.
9. Reduce oven heat to 350 and bake for 50–60 minutes.

Wayne's hint ☞ You can replace the pumpkin with sweet potato.

Orange Marmalade Poached Pears

6 hard Bartlett pears
2 cups of sugar
8 oz of orange marmalade
4 oz of Gran Marnier

1. Wash pears leaving stems on. Remove core from the bottom.
2. Place pears in medium saucepan and cover with water. Add sugar and bring to a boil.
3. Cook until fork can be inserted and easily removed.
4. Remove pears from pan and sit upright.
5. Using liquid in the pan add orange marmalade and Gran Marnier. Cook until liquid becomes syrup, about 10 minutes.
6. Place pears on a serving dish and pour syrup over them.
7. Garnish with fresh mint leaves or slices of oranges.

Wayne's hint ☞ I remove the core from the bottom with a melon scooper. It makes for a very easy way to core a pear.

Jean's Tupperware Pie Crust

Makes 6–8 shells

4 cups of flour
1 3/4 cups of shortening
1 Tbsp of salt
1 tsp of vinegar
1 Tbsp of sugar
1 egg
1/2 cup of water

1. Blend all ingredients together in a mixer.
2. Divide the dough out evenly (you should be able to make 6–8 shells with this dough which can be refrigerated or frozen until you decide to make another pie).
3. Roll the dough out between two sheets of wax paper.
4. Refrigerate crust for at least 30 minutes before filling.

Wayne's hint ☞ This recipe was given to Jean at her Tupperware party, henceforth, the name.

Jean Taylor's Brown Bag Apple Pie

Jean works at Angel's, a grocery store three miles up from Gibson Island on Mountain Road in Pasadena, MD. At first glance, you would think Jean was the sweetest, kindest, loveliest lady one could ever meet. For twelve years I thought that, until December 8, 2000 when she gave me this recipe. I rushed home to prepare the piecrust, (which I have never been able to conquer) and to bake this fascinating pie in a brown bag. After several phone calls to Jean at the store asking for guidance, I accomplished this dessert. I was so proud to have made a piecrust that didn't fall apart, and the bag trick made for one of the best-tasting pies ever. I had decided to add some cranberries and walnuts to the recipe. Sounds good, doesn't it? Well, when I went to the store the next day to tell Jean how successful I had been, I mentioned the walnuts and cranberries. She told me I had ruined her pie. The lady turned into a pie Nazi! It's been well over a year and every time, with a frown upon her face, she reminds me that I ruined her pie. I laugh and leave. It's just goes to show that baking is a passion, and I love Jean for being so protective.

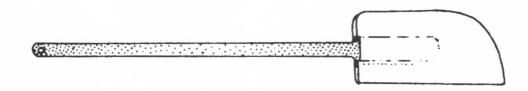

6 cups of apples, pared, cored, cut in half and then
   quartered
1/2 cup of granulated sugar
2 Tbsp of flour
1/2 tsp of cinnamon or nutmeg
2 tsp of lemon juice (optional)

Topping
4 oz of margarine, 1 stick
1/2 cup of granulated sugar
1/2 cup of flour

1. In a bowl, mix together 1/2 cup of sugar, 2 Tbsp of
   flour, cinnamon and lemon juice.
2. Stir apples in mixture until well coated.
3. Pour apples into prepared pie shell being sure you have
   refrigerated shell for at least 30 minutes.
4. In a bowl, mix together margarine 1/2 cup of sugar and
   1/2 cup of flour.
5. Cut mixture with 2 knives or pastry blender until
   mixture forms small beads (crumble).
6. Sprinkle crumble over apples.
7. Place pie into brown bag and seal with staples or
   straight pins.
8. Place on cookie sheet and bake at 425 for 60 minutes
   or until golden brown.

Wayne's hint ☞ The bag will not burn!

Cantaloupe Sherbet

I know a ten-year-old boy named Ben who loves to cook. I am always searching for easy but impressive recipes to give to him. This is one of those simple but great dishes that I can remember my mother preparing for us as children. I always thought that my mother had created every dish she ever made until I saw this recipe in an old cookbook dating back to the 1920s. Ever, since I can remember I have enjoyed reading old cookbooks, particularly those from the 20s, 30s and 40s. I've come to realize that many of the recipes we think we've created have been enjoyed for decades.

4 cups of cantaloupe (approximately), peeled, seeded
  and cut into 2 inch pieces
1/2 cup of sugar (more or less depending on how sweet
  cantaloupe is)
2 cups of milk

1. Place cantaloupe into blender (or mash with potato
   masher by hand).
2. Sprinkle sugar over top of the cantaloupe. Let stand for
   about two minutes.
3. Next, add milk.
4. Blend for about two to three minutes (just enough to
   chop cantaloupe).
5. Pour mixture into either three to four ice cube trays or
   one 9x11 Pyrex baking dish and freeze.
6. After frozen, place in a glass and serve with a sprig of
   mint.

Wayne's hint ☞ Other fruit can be used: strawberries, honey dew melon, blueberries, etc. For a special treat, try two or three fruits together.

Breakfast

Creamed Eggs with Asparagus and Bacon ▪▫▪▫▪▫▪▫▪▫▪

It's hard to get my nephew Gregory to eat anything, considering he dislikes most foods. But he loves creamed chipped beef. He spends a few weekends a month with me and I always ask, "What would you like for breakfast?" He grins like a Cheshire cat from ear to ear. I cringe because his smile means he will respond with, "creamed chip beef." So, after at least a hundred times of hearing his request, I decided to try something different. Using the same gravy, I chopped hard-boiled eggs, put it on toast points and garnished his portion with bacon and my portion with bacon and asparagus. I held my breath and delivered the goods. With a poker face, showing no emotion, I waited as he took his first bite. He looked at me, rolled his eyes, smiled a warm smile, and said, "My, this is good." It was a success. The cook was a success. The day was a success. Yes, another dish can be added to this ten-year-old's very short list of favorites.

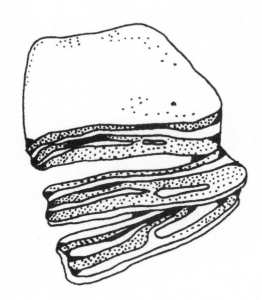

Serves 4

2 cups of milk or half-and-half
1/4 cup of butter
1/4 cup of flour
8 hard-boiled eggs, chopped
6 slices of bacon, cooked and crumbled
1/2 lb of asparagus, cut into 1/2 inch slices (optional)
8 slices of toast, white, whole wheat, or seven-grain cut
   into 4 pieces per slice

1. In a saucepan, melt butter, add flour and cook for 3
   minutes.
2. Gradually, add milk and bring to a boil to thicken.
3. Add chopped eggs and asparagus to cream mixture.
4. In a casserole dish, place toast pieces and top with
   creamed eggs.
5. Sprinkle bacon on top and serve.

Wayne's hint ☞ This recipe can also be served over biscuits. Your hard-boiled eggs can be made a day ahead of time.

The Irish Lady's Scones

On a visit to Ireland, I went to the Ring of Kerry where there was a farm high on a hill overlooking the Kenmare River. The reason Ireland is so green is the Gulf Stream and the trade winds that follow; they carry beautiful tropical warm air. It was January and everything from the vista was lush, with not even a hint of brown. The temperature was very moderate. The lady who owned the farm lived by herself in a two-room cottage. We enjoyed tea and scones with fresh dairy butter and homemade jam. She had recently purchased an electric stove. I was amazed to find out that prior to her new acquisition she had used a wood stove to make her scones. The year was 1998. The simplicity of her world, the beauty of the surroundings, and the foods she served created serenity that remains with me today, especially when I think of this recipe.

Serves 4

2 1/4 cups of flour(Flour will be different at different times of the time of the year, so you might need more or less.)
4 oz of margarine or butter, 1 stick, melted and cooled
1 cup of raisins
1 egg, slightly beaten
3/4 cup of milk or half-and-half
2 tsp of baking powder
1 tsp of baking soda
1/4 cup of sugar
1/2 tsp of salt

1. With a wire whisk, mix together flour, sugar, baking powder and salt.
2. Melt butter.
3. In a separate bowl, whip egg. Add milk, then butter and mix.
4. Add raisins to egg mixture.
5. Add wet and dry ingredients together. Mix thoroughly.
6. Turn dough onto lightly floured surface. (The consistency should not be tough nor should it be too wet it should be soft and pliable.)
7. Gently knead about 5–8 times.
8. Pat dough into a round shape, 1–inch thick.
9. Cut round into fourths.
10. Place on baking pan.
11. Brush with milk and sprinkle with sugar.
12. Bake at 425 for 15 to 20 minutes or until golden brown.
13. Serve with butter and jam or jelly.

Wayne's hint ☞ This makes four large scones. If you want smaller, cut it into eighths.

New York Apple Breakfast Cake ▰▰▰▰▰▰▰▰▰▰▰▰▰▰

New York is one of my favorite cities. It's my home away from home and always has been. I often said that wherever I found an apartment, there were three important things I needed from the neighborhood: 1. To be able to walk from the train station to the apartment (Have you ever try to get a cab in the rain in New York?). 2. Movie theaters, and 3. Probably the most important, a good bakery. For years I've checked out neighborhoods and their bakeries. Not so long ago I found a bakery not far from Union Square that served a breakfast cake made with pears. I asked for the recipe but it wasn't forthcoming. So I adapted a coffee cake recipe that we had used in the restaurant, and added apples. This is the recipe that was inspired by that New York bakery, even if they wouldn't give me their recipe (notice I don't mention the name).

Serves 4–6

The Cake
4 apples, cored, peeled, and cut into 1/2 inch slices
2 cups of sour cream
4 eggs
3 cups of flour, all-purpose
2 cups of sugar
4 tsp of baking powder
1 tsp of salt
The Streusel Topping
4 Tbsp of butter
4 Tbsp of flour
10 Tbsp of sugar
2 tsp of cinnamon

1. Grease 9x13 baking pan and place apples on the bottom.
2. Mix together flour, sugar, baking powder and salt.
3. In a separate bowl, blend sour cream and eggs.
4. Add all ingredients together and stir until smooth.
5. Pour over apples in baking dish.
6. Blend together butter, flour, sugar and cinnamon until it just crumbles. Do not over work.
7. Sprinkle crumbs over cake and bake for 1 hour at 350 or until knife when inserted into cake comes out clean.

Wayne's hint ☞ You can also use pears, which makes for a nice change.

Baked Eggs in Tomatoes

Serves 4

4 medium tomatoes
1/2 cup of breadcrumbs
1/2 cup of cheddar cheese, grated
2 oz of butter, 1/2 stick, cut into 4 pats
4 eggs
Salt and pepper to taste

1. **Cut the tops off of the tomatoes.**
2. **Remove pulp from inside of the tomatoes.**
3. **Slip one egg into tomato.**
4. **Salt and pepper.**
5. **Next, add a sprinkle of cheddar cheese.**
6. **Then, add a sprinkle of breadcrumbs.**
7. **Last a pat of butter.**
8. **Bake at 325 until breadcrumbs are brown.**

Wayne's hint ☞ Because you remove the pulp from the inside of the tomatoes, it is not necessary to wait until summer to make this recipe.

Baked French Toast

This recipe came from my sister Patricia. She loves this dish and so do I. I always like recipes that can be done in one dish and also made ahead of time. When people come over to enjoy your company it's nice to have most of the food already prepared so you can enjoy their company. The people you are with at mealtime are far more important than spending all your time in the kitchen. So, whenever possible try to find meals that you wish to share that are easy, simple and not time consuming.

Serves 6–8

4 granny smith apples, sliced and peeled
8 eggs
4 oz of butter, 1 stick
1 cup of brown sugar
2 Tbsp of corn syrup
1 loaf of French bread, 1/2-inch slices
1 tsp of vanilla
1 quart of milk
1/2 cup of raisins
1 tsp of nutmeg
2 tsp of cinnamon
1/2 cup of pecan or walnuts, chopped

1. **Heat butter, brown sugar and corn syrup until bubbly.**
2. **Pour into 9 x 13 pan. Arrange apples on top.**
3. **Sprinkle with nutmeg and cinnamon.**
4. **Layer slices of bread on top of apples.**
5. **Whisk together milk, eggs, and vanilla.**
6. **Pour over bread. Set in refrigerator overnight.**
7. **Bake at 350 for 45 minutes.**
8. **Sprinkle with raisins and walnuts and serve.**

Wayne's hint ☞ French bread can be substituted with sliced white bread, or, as I often do, sliced egg bread or Italian country.

Olaf Brokke's Buttermilk Pancakes

My father's cooking was scary at times, because he always made what he called soup from what ever was in the icebox (as he called the refrigerator) and always used barley to thicken his concoction. But every now and then (always on a Sunday) he would make pancakes—not just any pancakes, but his buttermilk pancakes. My mother would do the syrup, which was always heated. Sometimes, when we didn't have syrup, she would melt butter and add brown sugar. My favorite is buttery apple syrup—recipe listed below.

Makes 10–4inch cakes

2 cups of all-purpose flour
2 tsp of baking powder
1 tsp of baking soda
1 tsp of salt
1 Tbsp of sugar
2 eggs
2 cups of buttermilk
1/4 cup of vegetable oil
One banana

1. **Whisk together flour, baking powder, baking soda, sugar and salt.**
2. **In a bowl, whip together buttermilk, eggs and oil.**
3. **Combine dry and wet ingredients.**
4. **Blend in the bananas and mix well.**
5. **Heat a small amount of oil in a large skillet until a drop of water will bead.**
6. **Now you are ready to pour a spoon of mix on to the pan.**
7. **Cook until fluffy and brown and turn and cook other side, about 2–3 minutes on each side.**

Wayne's hint ☞ I like to double this recipe and put half the pancakes in the freezer. Whenever I'm in the mood for pancakes, I just pop one into a toaster oven.

Buttery Apple Syrup

4 oz of butter, 1 stick
1 cup of apples, peeled, cored and chopped small
3/4 cup of dark brown sugar
2 cups of apple cider or apple juice
1/4 tsp of cinnamon
1/4 tsp of nutmeg
1/4 tsp of salt
1 Tbsp of lemon juice
2 Tbsp of cornstarch

1. In a saucepan, melt 1/2 stick of butter. Save the other half for later.
2. Add apples and simmer for about 3 minutes.
3. Next, add brown sugar, cinnamon, nutmeg, salt and lemon juice.
4. Whisk cornstarch into apple juice.
5. Add cornstarch and apple juice to simmering apples.
6. Next, bring to a boil, then reduce to a simmer. Continue cooking for about 10 minutes.
7. Cut remaining butter into pats and add to syrup.
8. Stir and serve.

Wayne's hint ☞ You can refrigerate leftover syrup. When reusing, remember to heat.

Creamed Chipped Beef ▪▫▪▫▪▫▪▫▪▫▪▫▪▫▪▫▪▫▪▫▪▫▪

I have found that when kids help with the cooking they will usually eat what they make. This is one of those recipes that is ideal to get kids started in the kitchen. Gregory has been making this breakfast since he was eight years old. In fact, he thinks he created it. He really *did* create his own version of scrambled eggs when he was four. I encourage you to start your children early with simple, easy-to-make recipes. You will reap the benefits and so will they. You will get a helper in the kitchen, and they will become real cooks. Life lesson.

Serves 4

1/2 lb of chipped beef
2 Tbsp of butter or margarine
2 Tbsp of flour
2 cups of cold milk
1/4 tsp of nutmeg
Black pepper to taste

1. Melt butter and then add flour and cook for 5 minutes.
2. This makes a roux.
3. Slowly add cold milk to the roux.
4. Next, add pepper and nutmeg, salt may not be needed
   due to the salt in chipped beef.
5. Add the chipped beef, making sure that it is cut into
   bite-size pieces.
6. Serve over toast or biscuits.

Wayne's hint ☞ When making this for children, it helps if you cut the toast into fours first, then pour the cream chipped beef over the toast points.

The Grandmother's Maryland Oyster Pancakes

The Grandmother made oyster pancakes. I don't know if it sounds crazy to add oysters to pancakes, but we live in Maryland where oysters are second only to crabs. Where did she come up with this? I don't know—I've never seen it on a menu. I'm not sure if it was an extension of oyster fritters or a family recipe gotten from our relatives on the Eastern Shore. I never bothered to ask; I was always too busy enjoying Grandmother's oyster pancakes. These are great during Lent or on meatless Fridays. Serve with hot syrup or just butter. It might sound too sweet for this dish, but that's what my grandmother did. You should know that I called my grandmother "The Grandmother." This oddity fascinates Yvette, my assistant, so I should explain it now before you read the rest of this book. Grandmother was 4'11" or maybe even 5'. Since my late teens I have been 6'6". Her military demeanor, staunch presence, and fearless attitude always made me feel as though I was 4'11" and she was 6'6". Hence, The Grandmother, A.K.A. The General. My father would comment that he wished he could be half the man that she was when he grew up! Even on telephone calls I would say, "Hello, The Grandmother."

Serves 6

1 1/2 cups of all-purpose flour
1 Tbsp of baking powder
1 tsp of salt
1 Tbsp of sugar
2 eggs
1 cup of milk or buttermilk
1/3 cup of vegetable oil
1/2 pint of oysters, drained

1. Sift flour, baking powder, salt and sugar.
2. Beat together eggs, milk and oil.
3. Add dry to wet ingredients and stir.
4. Add oysters.
5. Heat large skillet until a drop of water will bead.
6. Cook until fluffy and brown then turn to cook other
   side.

Wayne's hint ☞ If you like corn, you can substitute it for the oysters.

Oven Shirred Eggs

Serves 3–6

6 eggs
12 Tbsp of half-and half
1 cup of cheddar cheese, grated
2 Tbsp of onion finely chopped
2 Tbsp of tomato, finely chopped

1. Preheat oven to 450 degrees.
2. Grease muffin pan or ramekins.
3. Put one egg in each cup.
4. Top each cup with 2 Tbsp of half-and-half
5. Sprinkle with a little onion and tomato.
6. Sprinkle with cheese.
7. Bake for 8 minutes do not over cook.

Wayne's hint ☞ Serve over toast points with a side of country ham or sausage.

Ham and Cheese Strata

This dish has always been ideal for my Brother Keith's family because I am never certain when they will arrive from out of town. Keith and Brenda (Brenda's the one who wore sunglasses while frying bacon so the grease wouldn't spatter and burn her eyes when she was first married at the age of 20), along with their three children, Jessica, Denis, and Karren, have lived in several states over the years. Sometimes they would travel together by car. At other times some would travel by car, the rest by plane. Why would they travel separately? I don't know. But you could always count on the fact that they would be home in Maryland for every holiday. How wonderful it is for children to see how important family is. If they stayed with me during one of their visits, I could never guarantee their time of arrival. I'm sure you have relatives like this. So, Ham and Cheese Strata came in handy for just this type of occasion. It can be made the night before. Just take it out of the refrigerator and put it in the oven. Sure makes breakfast easy.

Serves 6

12 cups of bread cubes (potato rolls works best)
8 eggs
2 quarts of half-and-half
2 cups of ham 1/4 inch cubes
1 1/2 cups of shredded cheddar cheese
Salt and pepper to taste
Butter for dish

1. Place bread cubes in a large mixing bowl.
2. Add ham and cheese and toss.
3. In separate mixing bowl, mix together milk and eggs.
4. Add salt and pepper.
5. Pour egg mix over bread, ham and cheese.
6. Let stand for one to two hours in the refrigerator.
7. Butter a 9 1/2 x 13 1/2, 2–inch deep baking pan.
8. Spoon mixture into baking pan.
9. Bake at 350 for 60–90 minutes or until golden brown.

Wayne's hint ☞ Recipe can be cut in half to accommodate your needs. Try substituting the ham with sausage.

Ms. Gladys's Fried Apples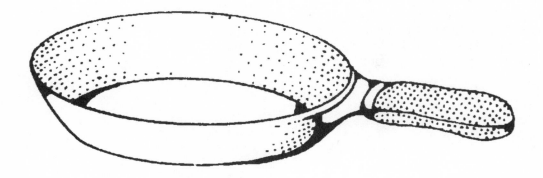

In the early days of running my first restaurant, my mother was always concerned about my eating habits. Without my knowing, she would call and instruct Ms. Gladys, a lady who cooked for fifteen years at my restaurant until she retired at the age of eighty, to feed me. This would inspire Ms. Gladys to surprise me with a glorious southern breakfast. She would show up in my office unannounced, with a plate overflowing with eggs, ham, and her wonderful fried apples. It was always a welcome surprise. Sometimes she would show up with a box containing various bottles of vitamins. I would ask her where they came from. Ms. Gladys would answer, "your mother sent them." Then she would say, "The man is still downstairs, it was sent C.O.D." Ms. Gladys and I would laugh and think of all the other things my mother would send C.O.D. She sent rugs for my housewarming, birthday presents, and the funniest of all, a singing telegram. After the lady in net stockings, top hat, and tails sang and danced to "Happy Birthday" with balloons in hand, she quietly asked to be paid. "Oh, and your mother said to tip me well."

Isn't it just wonderful how food is tied to memory?

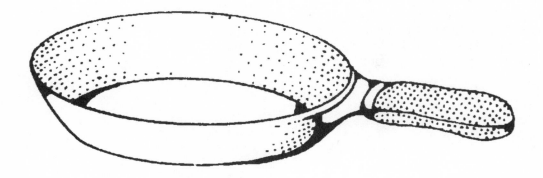

Serves 4
6 apples, cored and sliced
1 tsp of cinnamon
1/2 tsp of ginger
1 Tbsp of brown sugar, packed
2 oz of butter, 1/2 stick
1/4 tsp of salt
1/4 cup of water

1. **In a frying pan, melt butter. On medium heat, sauté apples until brown.**
2. **Next, sprinkle cinnamon, brown sugar, ginger and salt over apples.**
3. **Toss and allow apples to be coded and simmer for about 5 minutes.**
4. **If the apples are soft enough for you now, serve. If not, add water and simmer until you reach desired tenderness.**

Wayne's hint ☞ It's perfectly alright to leave the skin on the apple. If this recipe is too sweet, just add more apples.

Tex Mex Breakfast Casserole ▪▫▪▫▪▫▪▫▪▫▪▫▪▫▪▫▪▫▪▫▪

Located on Baltimore's Inner Harbor for the last twenty-one years, Wayne's Bar-B-Que is the only restaurant to serve breakfast on the waterfront. Folks from all over the world come to Baltimore to celebrate its great historic harbor. Foreign dignitaries, British royalty, and many other distinguished persons over the years have come to learn from this very successful urban project. I feel fortunate to have been a part of it. Breakfast, over the years, has evolved to include a variety of foods. The Tex Mex Breakfast Casserole and the Breakfast Burrito are some of the newest additions. Food, as fashion, changes with the times. The anthropologist Margaret Mead perhaps would have been interested to look into the evolution of restaurant menus. Then again, maybe not. . . . Who would have thought twenty years ago that oatmeal, cream of wheat, fried eggs, bacon, and a side of home fries would be replaced by a Tex Mex?

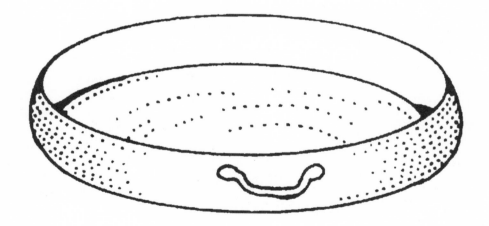

Serves 4

2 cups of day-old cornbread, crumbled
6 eggs, scrambled
1/2 cup of tomatoes, chopped
1/2 cup of green peppers, chopped
1/2 cup of onion, chopped
1 cup of grated cheddar cheese
Tortilla chips (approximately 20)
1/2 cup of sour cream
1 jalapeno pepper

1. Spread crumbled cornbread in an 8x8 baking dish.
2. Next, top cornbread with eggs followed by cheese.
3. Place dish in oven for 5 minutes or until cheese melts.
4. Then, remove from oven and place tortilla chips around exterior of baking dish, between the dish and cornbread.
5. Sprinkle with onions, tomatoes and green peppers.
6. Top with sour cream.
7. Next, slice jalapeno pepper into 1/8–inch slices and sprinkle over top.
8. Serve.

Wayne's hint ☞ This works best with cornbread. I can't think of any substitutions. If you need cornbread, we always have some available at waynecooks.com.

Potato Pancakes

I always thought potato pancakes had something to do with Lent or Easter. I grew up in a Catholic family and a mostly Catholic neighborhood. It wasn't until I was eighteen and went to work at a Hess Shoe Store in a predominantly Jewish neighborhood that I realized how important Potato Pancakes are to the Jewish faith. My grandmother's recipe was usually made with leftover mashed potatoes. Then I was delighted to find a wonderful cook and a lovely lady named Mary Tammers; she taught me how to make this dish with raw potatoes instead of leftovers. Mary would bring me baked goodies that she prepared for Jewish holidays. My favorite was hamantasch made with mun, poppy seed, that is usually prepared at Purim. Many years after leaving Hess Shoes, Mary Tammers, and the Jewish neighborhood, I was waiting tables in another part of town. I had a dream that woke me in the middle of the night with a craving for hamantasch. When I went to wait tables that night, I saw a Jewish family who were regulars of mine and told them the story of my dream. They all started laughing and said, "That's amazing Wayne, because it's Purim." I didn't even know.

Serves 4–6

2 lbs of potatoes, peeled and grated
1 carrot, peeled and grated
1 cup of onion, peeled and grated
2 eggs, lightly beaten
1 1/4 cups of bread crumbs
Dash of nutmeg
Salt and pepper to taste
1 Tbsp of lemon juice

1. **Toss grated onions and carrots with lemon juice to prevent discoloration.**
2. **Wrap in a clean dishtowel and squeeze out the liquid.**
3. **Place in a bowl.**
4. **Lightly beat eggs in separate bowl.**
5. **Add bread crumbs, salt and pepper and a dash of nutmeg. Mix.**
6. **Next, add potatoes and form into patties.**
7. **In a skillet, heat 1 inch of vegetable oil, add pancakes.**
8. **When the pancakes are golden brown, turn and brown other side, 3–4 minutes each side.**
9. **After frying, you can place in a 375 oven to become even crisper.**

Wayne's hint ☞ Flour can be substituted for the bread crumbs. You can also try substituting 1/4 of the potato with carrots or zucchini squash.

Herschel's Goop

Herschel was a cook who used to intimidate me. He could present a meal that looked as if it took days to prepare that actually took him only hours. When it came time for me to serve a meal to Herschel I was scared to death. It was my fortieth birthday and I had prepared a meal for friends. The entrée was curried crab cakes. I enjoyed them and it seemed that everyone else did as well. Several weeks later, I was having dinner with Herschel and his wife, Sally. I asked him if he enjoyed the curried crab cakes. His curmudgeon response was, "I only remember very good meals or very bad meals. I don't remember your curried crab cakes." That's why you won't find that recipe in this cookbook. I didn't get a compliment on my birthday meal that night, but I *did* get the scoop on Herschel's goop.

Serves 2 or one very hungry person

1 cup of oatmeal
2 cups of milk
1/2 cup of raisins
1/2 cup of walnuts or chopped pecans

1. In a bowl, mix together oatmeal, milk, raisins and nuts.
2. Cover the bowl and place in refrigerator over night.
3. In the morning you will have delicious cold oatmeal.

Wayne's hint ☞ The use of dried cranberries or cherries along with 1 Tablespoon of brown sugar makes for a wonderful variation on this dish.

Breakfast Potatoes

Most people know how to fry potatoes, so says Yvette. I would agree with her. My father would fry raw potatoes. My mother would fry leftover boiled potato. Both methods work, but I find raw potato sometimes needs a little help so, a trick I learned from a friend is to get the potato brown and if it's not fully cooked pop it in the microwave for a few minutes. You won't believe how great your potatoes will turn out

Serves 4

2 lbs of potatoes, peeled and cut into 2–inch cubes
1 lb of bacon, chopped and fried until crispy, drain and
 set aside
1 tsp of garlic
1 tsp of rosemary
1/4 tsp of red pepper flakes
1/4 tsp of paprika
1 cup of onion, chopped
1/2 cup of red sweet bell pepper
2 Tbsp of olive oil
Salt and pepper to taste

1. In a large skillet, place potatoes, cover with water and
 cook for about 10–15 minutes (until almost done).
2. Remove from pan, drain and set aside.
3. In same skillet with oil, add potatoes, cook until golden
 brown.
4. Then, add garlic, rosemary and red pepper flakes.
5. Next, add onions and red sweet peppers.
6. Add bacon and cook for about 3 minutes.
7. Arrange on platter and sprinkle with paprika.

Wayne's hint ☞ I like to add 1/2 cup green bell pepper while cooking. It won't make any difference if you don't use pepper at all. Leftovers the next day can be used for a potato omelet, topped with a little sour cream and chives.

Wayne's Cranberry Sauce

Seasons change and so do the foods that are associated with them. For me, cranberries conjure up cold weather. In early November, I buy cranberries and make this sauce. I put it in jars and place it in the refrigerator. Now, when I'm in the mood for a crispy toasted bagel slathered with cream cheese, I remove one of the jars and heap a large amount of cranberry sauce onto it. A cup of coffee, *The New York Times*, *The Baltimore Sun*—a routine that ten-year-old Gregory and I follow most Saturdays and Sundays (except he gets creamed chip beef or creamed eggs), and I'm happy, happy, happy. Sometimes I substitute pumpkin butter for the cranberry sauce. You can find the recipe in this book.

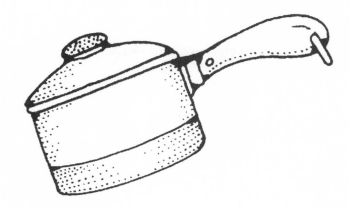

1 bag of fresh cranberries
1 cup of water
1 cup of sugar
Lemon juice from 1/2 a lemon
Orange juice from 1/2 a orange
1/4 cup of Grand Marnier
1 tsp of cinnamon
1 tsp of nutmeg
1 cup of walnuts
1/2 cup of raisins
1 cup of chopped apple

1. **Bring sugar and water to boil. Add cranberries and bring back to a boil then reduce to a simmer.**
2. **Next, add all other ingredients, cook for 10–15 minutes.**
3. **Remove from heat and allow to cool before serving.**

Wayne's hint ☞ Remember cranberry sauce is not just for Thanksgiving. It can be used as a breakfast jelly all year round.

Microwave Fresh Strawberry Jam ▪▫▪▫▪▫▪▫▪▫▪▫▪▫▪

This sounds too simple to be real. Well, I'm here to tell you, it is. I surprise myself every time I do this. I've made it with blueberries and blackberries. It's nice to have a hot, fresh jam. Microwaves were always, for me, to be used for popping popcorn and re-heating leftovers. More and more I am finding ways to make my life simpler and richer by the use of this not-so-new modern appliance. I had to stop being a snob about microwaves. I hope you've done the same.

2 cups of strawberries, rinsed, hulled and quartered
1/4 cup of sugar
1 tsp of lemon juice

1. **Place strawberries, sugar and lemon juice in a 6–cup microwave bowl.**
2. **Cook uncovered in microwave on full power until berry mixture is thick and spreadable, about 16 minutes.**
3. **Serve hot or cold. Store leftover jam covered in refrigerator.**

Wayne's hint ☞ This needs to be used right-away. It doesn't really keep well.

Cheddar Cheese Biscuit

2 cups of flour
2 tsp of baking powder
1/2 tsp of baking soda
1/2 tsp of salt
4 Tbsp of cold butter, cut into pieces
3 Tbsp of cold vegetable shortening (Crisco)
3/4 cup of buttermilk
1 cup of cheddar cheese

1. Place all dry ingredients in a large mixing bowl.
2. With a large whisk blend dry ingredients.
3. Cut butter and vegetable shortening into dry ingredients.
4. Add cheese.
5. Add buttermilk and stir with fork until dough forms into moist clumps.
6. Transfer dough into a floured work surface.
7. Form into a ball and with a rolling pin roll 1/2 inch thick.
8. Cut into 15 rounds.
9. Place on top of pot pie and bake at 375 for 25–35 minutes.

Wayne's hint ☞ I cut the butter and shortening with my fingers until butter is well incorporated into flour.

Wayne's Pumpkin Butter ▪️▪️▪️▪️▪️▪️▪️▪️▪️▪️▪️▪️▪️▪️▪️▪️

Like cranberry sauce, I like to make several jars of this early in November. It lasts for weeks if I don't eat it all at once. Again, I enjoy it on a bagel with cream cheese. This may sound terrible, but I like to put a large heaping tablespoon of Pumpkin Butter into a glass of cold, fresh milk—the taste gives me the sensation of Thanksgiving and satisfies my hankering for pumpkin pie. I also give Pumpkin Butter as presents. The Edwards family in New York—friends of mine—look forward with great anticipation to my gift. Try it . . . your friends will like it.

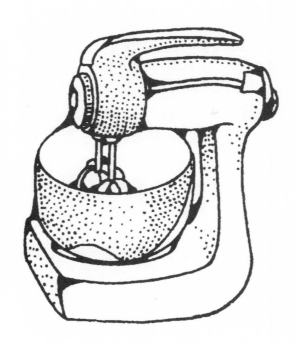

Serves 4–5

1–29 oz can of pumpkin
1 cup of dark brown sugar
1 cup of milk
1/2 cup of pecans, chopped
1/4 cup of molasses
1 Tbsp of lemon juice
1/2 tsp of ground nutmeg
1 Tbsp of cinnamon
1/2 Tbsp of ginger (or to taste)
1/2 tsp of coriander
1/2 tsp of salt

1. In a saucepan, on low heat add pumpkin.
2. In a bowl, mix milk and sugar together until sugar dissolves.
3. Next, add milk and sugar to pumpkin.
4. Then, add pecans, molasses, lemon juice, nutmeg, cinnamon, ginger, coriander and salt.
5. Cook on low heat for about 30 minutes stirring constantly.

Wayne's hint ☞ This will store for several weeks in your refrigerator.

Cool Summer Drinks

Ginger-Ale Punch

The very first time I was given ginger ale was at Aunt Molly's house. Whenever we would visit her, she would always have this special punch ready for us. I have always been amazed at how certain food and drinks can carry a person's life into the next generation. Aunt Molly was my great-aunt and neither Gregory nor his sister, Tamitra, has met her; but whenever I mention ginger ale they immediately respond, "Aunt Molly!" Aunt Molly is kept alive through this recipe in thought and in gratitude.

Pour six 12 oz bottles of Stewart's, Schwepps, or Canadian Club (a good ginger ale not in a liter bottle) into a punch bowl. Slide 1 pint of orange sherbet, whole, into ginger ale. Serve.

Orange Cooler

1. **Fill a glass with ice (crushed or cubed).**
2. **Fill 2/3 of the way with orange juice.**
3. **Fill 1/3 of the way with club soda.**
4. **Stir and Serve.**

Raspberry Cooler

1. Fill a glass with ice (crushed or cubed).
2. Fill 2/3 of the way with cranberry raspberry juice.
3. Fill 1/3 of the way with club soda.
4. Stir and serve.

Frappachino

Fill a glass 2/3 of the way with coffee (leftover morning coffee).
Fill 1/3 of the way with either half-and-half or milk.
Sweeten to taste.
Add ice, stir and serve.

Wayne's hint ☞ Another suggestion is to place all of the ingredients into a blender.

Peach Iced Tea (Any fruit)

1. Place 2 cups of fresh fruit into the bottom of a pitcher.
2. Put your hot tea on top of fruit.
3. Let it steep for about 45 minutes.
4. Strain and serve over ice.

Homemade Cherry Coke

1. Fill a glass 3/4 of the way with Coke
2. Add 2 Tbsp of Grenadine
3. Add 1 Tbsp of cherry juice
4. Add 3 cherries
5. Add ice, stir and serve.

Wayne's hint ☞ You can also use 7–Up. Can you imagine that?

Pink Lemonade

1. **For 2 quarts, add 6 lemons.**
2. **Sweeten to taste.**
3. **Add 2 Tbsp of Grenadine.**
4. **Add ice, stir and serve.**

Fruit Smoothie

1. **In a blender, place 2 cups of your favorite fruit.**
2. **1 cup of Yogurt**
3. **1 cup of either apple, pineapple, or orange juice**
4. **Fill with ice.**
5. **Blend and Serve.**

Kool-Aid Sangria

1. To cherry or grape Kool-Aid add 1 whole apple (cubed)
2. 1 orange
3. 1 lemon
4. Add ice, stir and serve.

Root Beer Float

1. Fill a glass 3/4 of the way with Root beer (Make sure Root beer is cold. Do not add ice).
2. Add 2 scoops of Vanilla Ice Cream.
3. Serve.

Frozen Hot Chocolate

3–6 oz packages of hot chocolate mix
2 cups of ice cubes
1 cup of milk, or as needed

1. Place milk, then chocolate, then ice into blender.
2. Add more milk if needed.
3. Serve in a tall glass.

Things Wayne Learned Along The Way

Weights and Measures

Liquid and Dry Measures

1 cup=1/2 pint

2 cups=1 pint=1 pound

2 pints=1 quart=2 pounds

4 quarts=1 gallon=8 pounds

16 ounces=1 pound

1 fluid ounce=2 Tablespoons

16 fluid ounces=1 pint

1 teaspoon=1/3 Tablespoons

1 Tablespoon=3 teaspoons

4 Tablespoons=1/4 cup

8 Tablespoons=1/2 cup

1 Tablespoon liquid=1/2 ounce

8 quarts=1 peck

4 pecks=1 bushel

Butter and Chocolate

2 Tablespoons butter=1 ounce

2 cups butter=1 pound

1 stick butter 1/2 cup

1 square baking chocolate=1 ounce

Miscellaneous Measures

1 cup grated cheese=4 ounces

4 cups coarsely chopped nuts=1 pound

2 1/3 cups uncooked rice=1 pound

1 cup uncooked rice=3 1/2 cups cooked

2 cups granulated sugar=1 pound

2 1/4 cups packed brown sugar= 1 pound

3 1/2 cups sifted confectioners sugar=1 pound

1 pound raw ground meat=2 cups

Substitutions ▪▫▪▫▪▫▪▫▪▫▪▫▪▫▪▫▪▫▪▫▪▫▪▫▪▫▪▫▪▫▪▫

If You're Out of This . . .	Use This . . .
Baking Powder, 1 tsp	1/4 tsp baking soda + 1/2 tsp cream of tartar OR 1/4 tsp baking soda + 1/2 cup of buttermilk or soured milk (reduce liquid in recipe by 1/2 cup) OR 1/4 tsp baking soda + 6 Tbsp molasses (reduce liquid in recipe by 1/4 cup and adjust sweetener)
Bread crumbs, dry, 1 cup	3-4 slices oven-dried bread, crushed OR 3/4 cup cracker crumbs OR 1 Tbsp quick-cooking oats
Broth, beef or chicken, 1 cup	1 cup boiling water + 1 bouillon cube, 1 envelope bouillon, or 1 tsp instant bouillon granules
Butter, 1 stick (1/2 stick)	1/2 cup (8 Tbsp) margarine OR 7 Tbsp vegetable oil
Buttermilk, 1 cup	1 cup plain yogurt OR 1 Tbsp vinegar or lemon juice + enough milk to equal 1 cup (let stand 5-10 min before using)
Chocolate, semisweet, 1 oz. (1 square)	1/2 oz. unsweetened chocolate + 1 Tbsp sugar
Chocolate, semisweet, 6 oz. chips, melted	9 Tbsp unsweetened cocoa powder + 7 Tbsp sugar + 3 Tbsp butter, shortening or vegetable oil
Chocolate, unsweetened, 1 oz. (1 square)	3 Tbsp unsweetened cocoa powder + 1 Tbsp butter, shortening or vegetable oil
Cracker crumbs, 1 cup	1 1/4 cups bread crumbs
Cream, half-and-half, 1 cup	1/2 cup light cream + 1/2 cup whole milk OR 1 Tbsp melted unsalted butter + enough whole milk to equal 1 cup

Substitutions ■▪■▪■▪■▪■▪■▪■▪■▪■▪■▪■▪■▪■▪■▪■▪■▪■▪■▪

If You're Out of This . . .	Use This . . .
Egg, whole, 1 egg	2 egg whites OR 2 egg yolks + 1 Tbsp cold water OR 3 1/2 Tbsp frozen and thawed egg OR 1/4 cup egg substitute OR 2 1/2 Tbsp powdered whole egg + 2 1/2 Tbsp water
Egg white, 1 white	2 Tbsp frozen and thawed egg white OR 1 Tbsp powdered egg white + 2 Tbsp water
Egg yolk, 2 yolks	1 whole egg (for thickening sauces) 2 Tbsp frozen and thawed yolk OR 1/4 cup powdered yolk + 4 tsp water (for baking)
Flour, all-purpose, 1 Tbsp (for thickening)	1/2 Tbsp cornstarch, potato starch, or rice starch OR 2 tsp arrowroot OR 1 Tbsp quick-cooking tapioca OR 2 egg yolks
Flour, all-purpose, sifted, 1 cup	1 cup minus 2 Tbsp unsifted all-purpose flour
Flour, cake, sifted, 1 cup	1 cup minus 2 Tbsp sifted all-purpose OR 1 cup minus 2 Tbsp sifted all-purpose flour mixed with 2 Tbsp cornstarch
Flour, self-rising, sifted1 cup	1 cup sifted all-purpose flour + 1 1/2 tsp baking powder + pinch salt
Lemon juice, fresh, 1 Tbsp	1 Tbsp bottled or frozen lemon juice OR 1 1/2 tsp white wine vinegar
Lime juice, fresh, 1 Tbsp	1 Tbsp bottled or frozen lime juice or lemon juice
Milk, whole, fresh, 1 cup	1 cup fat-free milk + 2 Tbsp butter or margarine OR 1/2 cup evaporated whole milk + 1/2 cup water OR 7/8 cup water + 1/4 cup dry milk OR 7/8 cup water + 1/4 cup nonfat fry milk + 2 1/2 tsp butter or margarine OR 1 cup soy milk

Substitutions

If You're Out of This . . .	Use This . . .
Milk, sour, 1 cup	1 Tbsp lemon juice or distilled vinegar + enough milk to equal 1 cup (let stand 5-10 min before using)
Mushrooms, fresh, sliced, 1/2 lb	4 oz. drained canned sliced mushrooms
Mustard, prepared, 1 Tbsp	1 tsp dry mustard + 1 tsp water
Onion, chopped, 1 medium	2 Tbsp jarred minced onion OR 1 1/2 tsp onion powder
Pecans, 1 cup	1 cup walnuts OR 1 cup rolled oats, toasted (for baking)
Raisins or dried currants, 1 cup	1 cup finely chopped soft prunes or dates
Sugar, confectioners, 1 cup	7/8 cup granulated sugar + 3 Tbsp molasses OR 1/2 cup dark brown sugar + 1/2 cup granulated sugar
Sugar, granulated, 1 cup	1 3/4 cups confectioners sugar OR 1 cup packed light brown sugar OR 1 cup superfine sugar
Sugar, light brown, packed, 1 cup	1 cup granulated sugar + 3 Tbsp molasses OR 1/2 cup dark brown sugar + 1/2 cup granulated sugar
Tomatoes, fresh, chopped, 2 medium	1 cup drained chopped canned tomatoes
Vinegar, distilled, 1 tsp	2 tsp lemon juice

Chart for Roasting ▪▪▪▪▪▪▪▪▪▪▪▪▪▪▪▪▪▪▪▪▪▪▪▪▪

Cut of Meat	Approx. min per lb. for 3–6 lb. roast
Beef (At 350°)	
Standing Ribs. . .Rare	26 minutes
Medium	30 minutes
Well done	35 minutes
Boned and Rolled Roasts increase cooking time	5–10 minutes
Pork (Fresh) (At 350°)	
Leg	45–50 minutes
Rib and Loin	35–40 minutes
Shoulder, Picnic	40 minutes
Shoulder (boned and rolled)	55 minutes
Shoulder, butt	40–50 minutes
Lamb (At 350°)	
Leg . . . Medium	35 minutes
Well–done	40 minutes
Crown . . . Well–done	45 minutes
Shoulder . . . well–done	35 minutes
Shoulder (boned and rolled)	40 minutes
Turkey	
8–10 pound cooked at 325°	3 to 3 1/2 hours
10–14 pound cooked at 325°	3 1/2 to 4 hours
14–18 pound cooked at 300°	4 to 4 1/2 hours
18–20 pound cooked at 300°	4 1/2 to 6 hours
Chicken	
4–5 pound cooked at 325°	2 1/2 to 3 hours
Over 5 pound cooked at 325°	3 to 4 hours

Other Things Wayne Learned Along the Way ▪▪▪▪▪▪▪▪

Frozen Vegetables
When deciding between fresh or frozen, I always prefer fresh. However, if you look at the ingredients on most frozen vegetable containers, you will see the only ingredient is the vegetable itself. So, when the vegetables are not in season, don't hesitate to use frozen. Sometimes frozen vegetables are of better quality because they are processed first, while the remainder is sent to market.

Herbs
Today, many people feel that fresh herbs are better than dried. I don't agree. I believe there is a time and use for both. Dried herbs are the most frequently used herbs in my recipes.

Dried Dried herbs should be kept in a dark and cool area. Herbs and spices usually have a shelf life of about one year. Keep an eye on the date and replace accordingly. I made a mistake and put parsley on my windowsill for easy access while I was cooking. After about one week, it turned yellow. I hope you can learn from my mistakes. Dried herbs are best used at the beginning of a recipe. This allows the herb to blossom with its flavor.

Fresh Fresh herbs can be placed into a glass of water and topped with a plastic bag or saran wrap. Put in the refrigerator, they should last for a week or so. I find that when using fresh herbs, they are best added towards the end of a recipe. This will insure that the intensity of flavor is not cooked away.

Fresh Basil Basil is in the mint family and gives off an aroma and flavor that will enhance many dishes. I think it's at its best when used with fresh tomatoes and salad dressings. It is also an enhancement for chicken, fish, and shrimp.

Dried Basil Dried Basil I have found that basil will bring out the flavor of asparagus in a soup. I also combine dried basil, marjoram, thyme, and rosemary to create what I call the Italian Four. This combination creates wonderful sauces and soups.

Thyme Thyme, dried or fresh, is the most wonderful accompaniment to chicken. For some reason you don't know it's there, but without it you know something's missing. It's one of the most frequently used herbs in my kitchen. For me it's like salt and pepper.

Sage This plant gives off a beautiful blue flower in early spring. The leaves themselves are only used at holiday time in my family. I find that combining fresh sage, mint, thyme, and rosemary with a little garlic and olive oil creates a wonderful dressing for meats. I use it to

Other Things Wayne Learned Along the Way :::::::::

top grilled chicken, shrimp, steak, or pork. I am not fond of marinades. This dressing compliments, but doesn't mask, the flavor of the meat.

Marjoram I use this herb primarily when I am cooking Italian food. It brings a wonderful sweetness to the dish.

Rosemary Not only is rosemary my favorite herb, I probably use it more often than any of the others. It's funny—I have basil, mint, oregano, sage, and thyme in my kitchen herb garden, but I find myself using rosemary the most. I love the pine fragrance. Through the winter, if it's not too cold, I still can snip sprigs and add to lots of dishes: roasted potatoes, mashed potatoes, dressings, stuffing, sauces and gravies, lamb, pork, beef, and shrimp all benefit from the use of this miraculous herb.

Dill Fresh or dried, dill can be used in a similar way. I also find that freezing dill does not change its texture. It is the only herb I freeze.

Mint I use it in drinks, salad dressings, soups, and meats. Please don't overlook this savory herb.

Temperatures

Ovens It's important to know your oven. When baking, it's very important. A few degrees one way or the other can make the difference between an under-cooked or over-cooked baked item.

Gas Vs. Electric I know a lot of people prefer gas and look down on people who use electric. It's kind of like sailboat people vs. powerboat people. I have had both gas and electric, and I think you eventually learn how to succeed with both. One thing I do, since I can't get natural gas where I live now, is: when I need to turn the heat down for a recipe, I just move the pot or pan to the side of the burner or take it off completely.

Pancakes

1. Don't overbeat.
2. Ignore the lumps.
3. If it's too thick add a little water.
4. If it's too thin add a little flour.
5. To keep the dough from sticking, add two extra Tablespoons of butter or oil.
6. Check griddle to see that it's ready by dropping a few drops of cold water one it to

Other Things Wayne Learned Along the Way ▨▨▨▨▨

see if it sizzles.
7. Don't drop batter from on high.
8. Cook for two to three minutes on each side.
9. Flip once.

Tuna

Always refrigerate your canned tuna. This will insure when you're ready to make your salad everything is at the proper temperature.

Eggs
Are They Fresh?

1. "Their shells should look dull . . . not shiny or bright; but it makes no difference if they're brown or they're white."
2. A fresh egg sinks when placed in cold water. Inside, the yolk is firm and upstanding; the white thick.
3. Chances that you are getting fresh eggs are greater if you buy from a stock that is refrigerated.
4. Place eggs immediately in the refrigerator—in the humidity-controlled section if you have one. Do not freeze!

When Cooking

1. When baking, always have eggs at room temperature.
2. Hard-boiled eggs—cover eggs completely in water. Do not pile eggs on top of one another. Bring to a boil. Remove from heat. Cover and let stand for 20 minutes.
3. Cooling Eggs—cool eggs under cold water. It makes it easier for shelling and also stops the cooking.

Other Things Wayne Learned Along the Way

Canned Goods VS. Fresh Produce

Fresh produce is seasonal, and like the change of seasons, enjoy and cook with what is available. Tomatoes are great only about three months out of the year, peaches maybe two months out of the year. The list goes on—I am talking about local produce, which I consider to be the best. With that said, canned tomatoes can and should be used when fresh tomatoes are not available, the same with peaches and other fruits.